Tony Abbott

Battlelines

MELBOURNE UNIVERSITY PRESS
An imprint of Melbourne University Publishing Limited
11–15 Argyle Place South, Carlton, Victoria 3053, Australia
mup-info@unimelb.edu.au
www.mup.com.au

First published 2009
Reprinted 2009
Updated edition published 2009
This edition published 2013

Text design by Phil Campbell
Typeset by TypeSkill

National Library of Australia Cataloguing-in-Publication entry:

Abbott, Tony, 1957–

Battlelines/Tony Abbott.

Updated Ed.

978522864423 (pbk.)

Bibliography

Abbott, Tony, 1957–
Liberal Party of Australia.
Politicians—Australia—Biography.
Conservatism—Australia.
Social prediction—Australia.
Australia—Politics and government—1996–
994.066092

To Louise, Frances and Bridget

Contents

Introduction

Political parties and their leaders need values and principles to sustain them. The quest for power must have a greater purpose than merely 'keeping us in and keeping them out'. *Battlelines* was partly personal story and partly political philosophy, but mostly it was my attempt to bring values tested by experience to the challenges our country faced.

For me, as for every leader of the Liberal Party, encouragement for the family, support for small business and respect for values and institutions that have stood the test of time are at the heart of my public life.

Battlelines was first published well before I became party leader. Any one person's vision, even the leader's, is necessarily tempered and refined by the passage of time and by the collective responsibility that is rightly at the heart of our political system. Still, it's worth republishing, now that our country is once more on the verge of choosing its government and its leader, so that Australians have the best possible chance to make an informed choice.

Late last year, the Liberal Party published a collection of my landmark speeches developing the Coalition's positive plans for a stronger and more prosperous economy and for a safe and secure Australia. Earlier this year, the party released our Real Solutions Plan for Australia, which assembled the specific policy commitments that the Coalition has already made for the coming election. These are available to download at www.liberal.org.au.

Unlike them, *Battlelines* is not an official party document. It didn't undergo the consultation and refinement of a major speech by a party leader. It wasn't directed to an immediate political challenge or opportunity. It was my personal attempt to grasp a post-Howard vision for my party and for the conservative side of politics as well as an element in renewing my personal commitment to public life in the aftermath of a wrenching defeat.

Obviously, there were some proposals in *Battlelines* (such as the referendum to give the Commonwealth more authority over the states) that were the product of Howard-era frustrations with hostile state governments. The past five years have been a good antidote to the view that political wisdom mostly resides in Canberra. As well, Coalition rule in the big states means that an incoming Coalition government in Canberra should have more willing partners with whom to work.

There were suggestions in *Battlelines* for a tax cut for families with dependent children and also for a Medicare-style system of dental rebates that should not be considered until the Commonwealth budget is again in strong surplus. There was also the suggestion of a fundamental reconsideration of the way retirement savings might be handled that would not be practical given the way the superannuation system has become entrenched. There was also a fleeting consideration of 'covenant marriage' that I would no longer support.

Since *Battlelines* was published prior to the last election, WorkChoices has been killed, buried and cremated. The past is the past and we will never go back to it. The fundamental problem with the former government's policy in this area was that it broke faith with the 'Howard battlers', who felt betrayed by changes for which no mandate had ever been sought. For the coming election, the Coalition's workplace policy will be careful, cautious, responsible change within the framework of the Fair Work Act, focused on solving practical problems rather than applying economic theory.

On the other hand, *Battlelines*' proposals for community-managed public hospitals and for independent public schools drew on the work of the Kennett government in Victoria and of the Barnett government in Western Australia. Should the Coalition win this year's election, it would be relatively easy to negotiate a way forward on these with the states.

Battlelines' contention that there's a relatively happy marriage between liberalism and conservatism thanks to a long tradition of freedom in Westminster-derived polities has, in my judgment, been vindicated by the relative absence of internal party ideological disputes over the past few years.

I hope *Battlelines*' latest readers will notice a substantial unity and coherence between my thinking in 2009 when the book came out and the policy commitments that the Coalition has made since I became leader. Over the years, I have changed my mind on some vexed questions (such as multiculturalism and paid parental leave) but this is because I have reconsidered the application of principles, not changed them.

A preference for freedom, for trusting people to get most things right most of the time, and for individuals knowing their best interests better than officials do, pervades all the Coalition's significant policy commitments.

The difference between the Coalition and its opponents is not that one side supports a fair go for the vulnerable and the other doesn't. The contest is not between one party that is moral and another that isn't. I am a Liberal because I'm convinced that it's our policies—rather than Labor's—that will most effectively produce the fairer, freer and more prosperous society that almost every Australian wants.

With more than 2 million more jobs, a 20 per cent–plus increase in real wages, and a doubling of real net wealth per person, the Howard government could justly claim to have had the best interests of workers at heart. What's more, our party is much more broadly based than the contemporary Labor Party, which has been colonised by an apparatchik class of former union and party officials.

As liberals, the Coalition supports lower taxes, smaller government and greater freedom. As conservatives, we support the family and values that have been proven over time. As pragmatists, we support policies that pass the common-sense test and that can reasonably be expected to make our country stronger: hence, my occasional description of the Coalition's political philosophy as 'pragmatism based on values'.

The main policy commitments of an incoming Coalition government are already clear. We will:

- abolish the carbon tax, because that's the quickest way to reduce power prices and take the pressure off the cost of living
- abolish the mining tax, because that's the quickest way to boost investment and jobs
- fund a tax cut without a carbon tax through dispensing with unnecessary bureaucracies and programs that involve second-guessing other levels of government
- cut red-tape costs by at least $1 billion a year, to give small business a much-needed break
- return the budget to a sustainable surplus, because cutting unnecessary spending means more money for the spending that's really needed
- establish a fair-dinkum paid parental-leave scheme that pays nearly all mothers their actual wage for six months, because it's a workplace entitlement, not a welfare one
- create two million more jobs within a decade by restoring the jobs growth of the Howard government
- stop the boats by restoring the border protection policies that have been proven to work
- make the work of government more effective and efficient through a once-in-a-decade commission of audit
- set up a root-and-branch review of competition policy to ensure that small business gets a fair go
- revitalise work for the dole
- within twelve months start work on Melbourne's East–West link, Sydney's WestConnex, Tasmania's Midland Highway upgrade and Brisbane's Gateway motorway upgrade, as well as other key roads in Adelaide and Perth

- duplicate the Pacific Highway, finally, well within this decade
- reduce emissions by planting more trees, delivering better soils and using smarter technology rather than a carbon tax, which just sends our jobs overseas
- establish a one-stop shop for faster environmental approvals so that new projects can get up and going more quickly
- fully restore a tough cop on the beat—the Australian Building and Construction Commission—to deliver (as it previously did) at least $5 billion a year of productivity improvements in a troubled industry
- provide the same penalties for union officials and company officers who commit the same offence
- move towards community-controlled public schools and hospitals run by local leaders, not distant bureaucrats, so they're more responsive to the parents and patients they serve
- implement a new Colombo Plan to provide a two-way street between Australia and our region, sending our best and brightest to study in the region and bringing their best here
- make childcare more responsive to the 24/7 needs of today's working families through a swift but comprehensive review of the current system
- make no unexpected changes that are detrimental to people's superannuation
- impose no further reductions in defence spending, which has already fallen to the lowest level, as a percentage of GDP, since 1938
- at least maintain spending on health and medical research, where Australia's talented scientists give us such a comparative advantage.

These are affordable, achievable, and sensible measures that the Coalition could deliver or at least substantially begin in a first term. Each one of them is driven by our preference for a smaller government with more citizen participation leading to a more prosperous and better respected Australia.

If elected, my expectation is that Australians will swiftly notice not just a new government with different policies, but also a different way of governing, with far more respect for the people that government policies affect. Government can't please all of the people all of the time, but it can and should take them into its confidence on the issues that will make a difference to their lives.

Effective decision-making involves the assimilation of a range of advice. It's not simply doing what one set of experts advises. It's not simply picking the most authoritative of competing sets of advice either. Effective decision-making is neither contracted out nor conducted in isolation or on the run. It involves engaging with the relevant interest groups and assimilating their arguments prior to making a decision. Crucially, it should also involve testing a potential course of conduct with the people it will impact upon before any decision is actually finalised.

The next Coalition government won't shirk hard decisions, but will talk to people before decisions are made rather than just argue with them afterwards. As those who have worked with me as a minister can attest, my style is to consult with the people that a government decision could impact upon and to work out for myself what are its real pros and cons. The next Coalition government won't take a 'we know best' approach and will seek a more rational and wider-ranging public debate about the problems our nation faces and the best means to resolve them.

Over the past two years, the Coalition has spent much time criticising the government because, let's face it, there has been much to criticise. It's the Opposition's job to call out incompetent administration, broken promises and misconceived policies. Still, criticism of a bad government, if that's all there is, can lead to a pretty dispiriting national conversation.

Essentially, voters have to answer two questions in deciding to change the government: the first is whether the existing government deserves to lose; the second is whether the current Opposition deserves to win.

Oppositions, therefore, have two tasks: the first is to persuade people to vote against the incumbent; the second is to persuade people to vote for the alternative. Both are vital because bad governments quite often get re-elected by sowing doubts about the opposition.

As demonstrated back in 1998, Australians are prepared to support a government that has genuinely taken tough decisions. What they very rarely forgive is a government that makes promises before an election to win votes, but abandons them afterwards to hold power. Notoriously, the Keating government dumped its L-A-W-law tax cuts in 1993 in a betrayal that haunted that government to its political grave, just as the 'no carbon tax under the government I lead' promise now haunts Prime Minister Gillard.

True believers aside, the current government now has very few defenders. Clearly, it's been incompetent and untrustworthy. Given Labor's failure, the issue is the extent to which the current Opposition can be trusted to do better. With sixteen shadow ministers who have already been ministers in a much better government than the present one, I am confident that things can be so much better than they are now.

This is a great country and we are a great people, let down by a bad government in Canberra. There is almost nothing wrong with our country that a change of government wouldn't improve. That's why I am so convinced that our best years as a nation are ahead of us and why I am so determined to give Australians the better government that we all deserve.

My political thinking will continue to evolve for as long as I am in public life. *Battlelines* remains, nevertheless, a key milestone in its development.

1 The Making of a Liberal Politician

The brutal searchlight on politics and politicians really caught me one morning in February 2005. I was at the Adventist Hospital in Sydney to make a ministerial announcement. There was a forest of boom mikes and swarms of journos who wouldn't normally go near a health launch. The heaving scrum was not there to talk about policy but to grill me about an old love and a new-found son.

Kathy had been my first girlfriend. She was funny, clever, artistic and charismatic. At nineteen, we had been deeply in love. There was one problem, though. A part of me said that I should join the priesthood. So our romance was on-again, off-again and in the weeks when we were an item rather than 'just friends' we played what used to be called Vatican roulette.

One day, she tearfully announced that she was pregnant. For us, an abortion was out of the question. At first, we were going to be married. Then I got cold feet. I was too young and, frankly, too confused for that responsibility. She didn't think she could bring up a child on her own so decided that the baby should be adopted. I had let her down, badly, so after the birth we went our separate ways. Still, we'd remained friends, stayed in touch and often wondered what would happen if our baby made contact. My reaction, I always felt sure, would be to 'dissolve into unmanly tears'.

Since July 1977 the unknown son had been a part of my life. It wasn't something that I regularly discussed or even thought about on a daily basis, but it was part of my self-understanding. In 1983, when I finally did begin to train for the priesthood, I had needed to explain that I hadn't always been able to live up to the ideals of the faith. In 1987, when I met my wife-to-be, Margie, and was inviting her to share a future, I had to warn her that she might meet a child who wasn't ours. It was a minor talking point around Canberra too. My parliamentary sparring partner, former Labor MP and one time leader, Mark Latham, used occasionally to interject, especially when industrial relations was my topic, 'you've had too many unions, Tony, you grub'.

Just before Christmas 2004, Kathy called to say that Daniel had made contact and was on his way to meet her and her family in Western Australia. I spoke to Daniel and arranged for him to meet my family too. There was excitement and awkwardness. My sisters reckoned that there wasn't much family resemblance. Late in January 2005, the editor of *The Bulletin* called to say that he was aware of the reunion and was going to run a story. Eventually, there was a furious race to break the news and a 24-hour media frenzy.

About a week later, Kathy called again, distraught, to tell me that a 1976 flatmate had been in touch to claim that Daniel might be his. One night, apparently, there'd been a party. She'd come home late, her room was occupied, so she'd shared her flatmate's bed. It was a blurred memory that she'd never mentioned before because she had been so certain that Daniel was mine—perhaps, she said, because she had so wanted Daniel to be mine.

When the test result came back, I don't know who was more shattered: Kathy because she had misled someone she'd loved, or me because, after twenty-seven years wondering, I'd found someone else's son. Still, having lost a child, I wasn't going to lose a friend as well. Anyone can make a mistake. How you deal with it is the true test of character. The gutsiest interview I have ever watched was Kathy facing up to the mistake on Channel Nine. Of course, it was the connection with me that meant she had to go through that excruciatingly public ordeal.

Because I was a politician, what would have been a personal issue and a family matter for those immediately concerned became a minor soap opera. As a politician, I had more or less learned to cope with living in a goldfish bowl. In this case, though, my former girlfriend, her son and my wife became the objects of public speculation and gossip because of their connection with me. It was an illustration of the toxic side to politics. Politicians are volunteers. They choose their life. Families are conscripts. Exposing your family to public notice is part of the inescapable downside of being in public life.

In an important sense, I owe my wife, my children, Kathy, Daniel and everyone closely connected with me a deep debt. Because I am in public life, they are too. My foibles might be considered fair game. Theirs should not be but are thanks to insatiable media and the inclination to turn public figures into actors in a morality play. Last year, for instance, a sideline incident at the under-tens northern suburbs netball grand final became a radio talking point for no other reason than it involved 'Tony Abbott's sister'. Because her fifteenth birthday party attracted some would-be crashers, *A Current Affair* wanted to interview my daughter for national television.

Public life can be deadly for families. Politicians' spouses and children are (often incorrectly) assumed to share their views, inevitably get dragged into their fights and invariably are tarred with the same brush. They get caught in the searchlight even when it's not aimed directly at them. All too often, family events are hijacked by political developments or have to be planned around the local branch barbecue or RSL dedication. It's no wonder that some political spouses feel 'ripped off'.

Since I became a member of parliament, Margie has had to run the household and organise our children's lives mostly on her own. In recent years, she's also held down a busy and responsible job. Although her life would have been much easier but for the career choices that I have made, she has always supported me in my work. One morning, noticing a headline about the circumstances of former MP John Brogden's departure from the state Liberal leadership, she warned: 'whatever happens, don't you say anything about it'. Foolishly,

I did not entirely heed this advice and spent weeks publicly apologising and trying to explain.

Margie reckons that she first questioned my suitability as a potential partner on our second night out when, apparently, I had expected her to discuss the continuing aftershocks of the political upheavals of the 1950s. On our honeymoon, we'd spent three days sailing near Stradbroke Island in Queensland. Every morning, we had to work the boat off the sandbanks on which I'd stranded it as the tide went out overnight. As the yacht finally gyrated down the Broadwater under a stiff nor'easter and a badly managed 'goosewing' rig, her hands bleeding from pulling on unfamiliar ropes, Margie asked whether I always did things the hard way!

Even the toughest MPs sometimes wonder whether political life is worth the personal cost. Judging by politicians' divorce rate, their spouses often conclude that it's not. The hours are killing, the rewards modest, the responsibilities daunting, the exposure relentless, the gratitude uncertain, and the strain imposed on family members quite unfair. The rigours are more intense because almost no one outside politics fully appreciates them. Yet someone has to represent an electorate in parliament, help lead political parties and take responsibility for decisions about the future of our country. If you want to make a difference, it's the price you've got to pay.

Australians shouldn't feel sorry for politicians. Still, if they understood the nature of political life, they might be less incorrigibly critical. If politics were just another job, almost no one would take it. If politics were a 'career' that people might enter for money, interest or lifestyle, almost no one would stay in it. Any true vocation involves something akin to love. Military personnel, for instance, would not put their lives on the line; health professionals would not continue to deal with demanding patients, or teachers work with difficult students, without a passionate belief that what they did really mattered—that it's an end in itself. Unless people's hearts are in the hard tasks, no level of remuneration or kudos can compensate for the challenges and risks involved.

There's an element of paradox in politics, as in other vocations. A soldier must want peace but prepare for war. A police officer must fight crime but mix with criminals. A teacher must have a passion for learning but endless patience with the ignorant. In a similar vein, a politician has to be a leader but cannot be a dictator. Politicians have to stand out in some way but also have to be 'of the people'.

In at least one important respect, though, politics is harder than most other vocations. Australians normally profess to respect soldiers, police and teachers. They don't generally admit to respecting politicians; quite the opposite, in fact. 'To the prick on "Lateline"' was the salutation on an email I received recently (addressed to me rather than the interviewing journalist!) from someone claiming to be a staunch Liberal voter but upset over something I'd said. The members of other vocations do not normally face the personal vitriol and public exposure that politicians have to take for granted.

Politicians live on a public stage but without the leeway that is sometimes extended to celebrities. Occasionally, when a politician is on a roll, faults are explained away. More often, though, no benefit of the doubt is given. Kevin Rudd's visit to a 'gentlemen's club' in New York was excused on the grounds that 'everyone's human'. Mostly, though, politicians who have a significant lapse of judgment or a moral flaw at the very least become pariahs-de-jour for a critical public.

Scrutiny is a necessary part of politics, but its intensity and unforgiving nature are among the reasons most people find the prospect of public life so uninviting. No one can ever be entirely ready for its humiliating rituals, such as 'are you a fool or a knave?' cross-examinations from the media or the occasional 'you have ruined my life' accusation from an unhappy constituent. It's understandable that cancer sufferers, for instance, desperate to get a new drug on the Pharmaceutical Benefits Scheme, would try moral blackmail on health ministers who have to stand up for rigour in decision-making. Only prime ministers normally have to wear the accusations of blood on their hands from grief-stricken relatives, as John Howard did after Bali. Still, this kind of pressure is what leads the public to conclude that politicians would have to be slightly crazy to want the job.

Most politicians are a mix of idealism and ambition. The highly driven and the deeply idealistic individuals who enter public life all have a personal story. That story helps to explain the positions they adopt and the decisions they take. Understandably, people want to know whether the person seeking their vote is fair dinkum. Their personal histories nearly always cast light on their public life. All of us are the product of the people, institutions and cultures that we have lived among. We aren't 'programmed' by experience, but we're certainly shaped by it.

In an essay for *Quadrant*, the British conservative thinker Roger Scruton says that our own self-respect requires us to respect our culture and its institutions. This, he says, 'is the first maxim of conservative politics: self-respect requires respect for institutions; to the extent that we learn a habit of mockery towards our inheritance, to that extent do we mock ourselves'.[1] The second task of the conservative, he says, is to 'give up this breast-beating, guilt-ridden desire to throw away our inheritance'.[2] Indeed, I have often pondered the psychology of people who seem uncomfortable with the society that has formed them. There is much about Australia that I would like to change, but not its fundamentals. How could I, given the extent to which it's made me what I am?

My parents had two messages for their children: first, 'be as good as you can be at whatever you do', and, second, 'we love you whatever happens'. Of course, there was not too much 'kids will be kids' tolerance when, for instance, some devilry drove me and the neighbouring children, as eight-year-olds, to carve our names into the duco of the cars in the street. Still, while I was growing up I never had the impression that my parents were mad at me rather than about my (fairly frequent) misdeeds.

For several years of my childhood, every weekday, I walked the couple of kilometres or so from home to Chatswood railway station with my dad before the train ride to school. I can only remember the odd snatch of conversation, which, I'm sure, would have been about trivia as well as the things that were going on in my life. I do very clearly recall, though, Dad's insistence that it was better to be a good man than a successful one. Later, when I felt 'out of it' at a new high school, I vividly remember him consoling me with the advice that if I learned to like others they would eventually find something to like in me.

Both my parents taught by example. From Mum, I learned that the ideal home welcomes people and makes them feel part of the family. From Dad, I learned that you should always look for the best in others and try to be for them what you would have them be for you. That doesn't mean that life in the Abbott household was a re-run of 'The Brady Bunch'. It seems to be the nature of the parent-child relationship that there's always so much more that ought to be said. Still, I could not have asked for a better start and for more ongoing encouragement. Mum and Dad were the best type of parents, nearly always thinking well of their children, sometimes to the point of imagining that we're better than we really are.

As best I can remember, my interest in public life first stirred as a child reading the Ladybird books that my Mum brought home. These usually turned out to be about great figures in history: Julius Caesar, Francis Drake and Henry V are three that I seem to recall. The lesson, invariably, was that duty and honour carried the day. They were caricatures, of course, as I was to discover over time, but uplifting ones. In the real world, good doesn't always triumph and justice doesn't always prevail. Even the best turn out to have their flaws. Despite that, ideals don't cease to matter because they're never perfectly achieved or because their adherents are compromised.

In those days, the mid-1960s, 'history' started with the Greeks and the Romans before focusing on the story of England and Britain's influence on the world. Not surprisingly, I became an admirer of parliamentary democracy, freedom under the law, and liberal institutions. As these were largely made in England (although often improved elsewhere), I also became an incorrigible Anglophile.

I was born in London while my father was studying for a specialist qualification, then not available in Australia. When I eventually went back to England as a student, I didn't feel that I was visiting a foreign country, despite the passport queues at Heathrow airport. As I flew over the city of London, it felt like more than a homecoming. The metropolis was not just the inspiration for a Monopoly board but the chief source of the language I spoke, the centre of the system of law I lived under and the fountain of the democracy I cherished.

It belonged to me as much as to any Briton. 'Beating the Poms' is as important to me as to any other Australian, but it's like wanting New South Wales to beat Queensland in the rugby league state of origin series. Only on the sports field are the British an alien tribe. Indeed, it would be a very rare Australian, I suspect, who feels like a stranger in any English-speaking country regardless of disagreements that might exist between governments or about policy.

Apart from my parents, the church was the biggest influence on my early life. From 1966 till 1975, I was at St Aloysius and then St Ignatius College, Riverview, in Sydney. The college mottos, 'born for higher things' and (roughly translated) 'do as much as you can', give a good idea of the Jesuit ethos at that time, which I thoroughly assimilated, sometimes to my masters' annoyance.

In year twelve I wrote a precocious essay concluding that Riverview would be a better school if it turned out the future leaders of society as well as good professional men. To the best of my recollection, the offending sentence had to be removed for the essay to appear in a school publication. When one of my classmates was not made a prefect—unfairly I thought, because of his involvement in a silly prank—a friend and I lobbied all the other prefects to have this injustice rectified. In one-on-one discussion with us, everyone agreed to support our position. In the subsequent round-table meeting with the headmaster, no one else did.

In October 1975, the then governor-general, Sir John Kerr, presented the prizes at the school's speech day. A routine vice-regal engagement turned out to have fallen in the middle of an unprecedented political struggle in which the governor-general would be umpire. When it was my turn to shake Sir John's hand, I said that I had a car outside to take him to the Liberal Party rally in town. He took the joke in good part, but the school authorities thought I had made a spectacle of myself. Years later, perhaps to prevent some similar lapse, John Howard did all the talking during my one and only presentation to the Queen.

On more than a few occasions, high spirits, exuberance, and sometimes—yes—overindulgence have landed me in considerable trouble. At the end of my second year at university, challenged at a public meeting by a fellow platform speaker about where I stood on an issue (I was standing behind her), I touched her on the back and made a facetious remark. She claimed that I'd indecently assaulted her, and a criminal charge went to court, where it failed. After a big night out in my fourth year of university, a squad car observed me trying to bend over a street sign in a test of strength with a fellow student. This time, I pleaded guilty, but no conviction was recorded. After a particularly riotous Queen's College middle common room dinner, a mate and I detoured through Magdalen College on the way home and did a little late-night gardening. Filled with remorse as the enormities of the previous evening seeped back, I slunk into that blessed plot late the next morning in time to see the long-suffering college gardeners repairing the last of the damage. At least I had been finally cured of the impulse to break things.

One virtue that the Jesuits never quite managed to inculcate in me was humility. It was probably good for me not to be picked for all the sporting teams or leadership positions that I aspired to. Sometimes, life wasn't fair. Then again, often it was, but I lacked the magnanimity to appreciate the fact. I have always wanted the institutions that I identified with to be at their best and have not always recognised how failings could be mine rather than theirs. In response to some schoolboy complaint of mine, my paternal grandfather once recalled a lesson from his own school days: 'the reason is hidden in a pattern that God has planned. If we believe and trust in him, some day we will understand'. I can only remember this, I suspect, because I find it hard to accept.

The Jesuits who taught me wanted to bring out the very best in their students but didn't expect them to be saints. They weren't disloyal to the Pope or subversive of the church but often seemed impatient with the 'scold' side to religious teaching. 'Don't bother giving up chocolates for Lent', Father Emmet Costello used to advise, 'but do something positive like going to Mass more often'. 'We are all the products of those who have loved us or failed to love us', he often observed, quoting, I think, the American Jesuit John Powell. For me, the message was that God preferred big-hearted people who might sometimes make mistakes rather than robotic rule worshippers. In the hands of the

Jesuits, to be Catholic meant to 'have life and have it to the full'. They seemed to have worked out that fire and brimstone was more likely to cut people off from the church than to frighten them into better behaviour. Their message was that you can't condone sin but you can usually understand why it happens.

Even though the Jesuits weren't much fussed about rote learning the catechism, at least in those days, their charges mostly seemed to assimilate the greatest Christian truths: to love God with your whole heart and to love your neighbour as you love yourself. This second commandment is rightly the whole basis of human ethics. 'What would you want if the boot was on the other foot?' provides the best answer to so many moral dilemmas. The social teaching stemming from this reflected, it has always seemed to me, not some Vatican diktat but the best human instinct.

Taking the church seriously doesn't mean that I have always found its commandments easy to keep. At home and at school, for instance, I'd always been taught that sex was special and that it should be for marriage. That was fine until I met the most fascinating person in my life up till then, who happened to be a girl. Awkwardly, it was just as Kathy and I became more and more involved that I started to think more seriously about the priesthood. To love a woman intensely and at the same time to want to love God more didn't strike me as odd, just very messy for a pair of unmarried Catholics.

To the best of my recollection, the first stirring of a political commitment had come in 1972, when my year nine history teacher set an essay on the policies of the parties contesting that year's election. For some reason, I watched the Democratic Labor Party policy launch, as well as those of the big parties. Vince Gair had no charisma and little subtlety, but I liked his party's support for traditional values as well as its support for workers within a market economy.

In those days, just two decades after the Labor Party had split over the role of Catholic Action in the campaign against communist union leaders, quite a few Catholic school headmasters still sympathised with the work of BA Santamaria. Some used to suggest the names of school leavers to be invited to conferences about university life. When a school friend received an invitation, I was only too happy to provide him with company.

That conference helped to channel my Jesuit-inculcated desire to be 'a man for others' into an immediate political outlet. It was a thrill to meet people of influence and authority in public life. It was exciting to think that I might be able to make a difference to the wider world. Most of all, it was good to learn that there was a way to get involved immediately through joining the Sydney University Democratic Club. This was the successor to the former DLP club and was supported and sustained by Santamaria's National Civic Council.

At that time, Santa had been a political crusader for forty years, a public intellectual much loved and greatly loathed in almost equal measure. Only in retrospect can I dimly appreciate the degree of commitment to a cause that led him to take so much trouble over potential recruits. What impressed me, even as a youth, was the courage that kept him going as an advocate for unfashionable truths. He always seemed more concerned for the cause than for himself.

Although he befriended many Liberals, Santamaria retained a lifelong reticence about the party of capital, as he saw it. Years later, he declined to give me a preselection reference. I think he feared that I just might win and that he would have to adjust his prejudice that serious Catholics couldn't advance in the Liberal Party. As it happened, John Howard was almost his last visitor and I obituarised that the 'DLP is alive and well and living inside the Howard Government'. If I ever proposed new spending measures or had a good word for unions in cabinet, former treasurer and deputy leader Peter Costello would jocularly enquire whether I was 'channelling Santa again'.

The following year, 1977, I joined the Sydney University Liberal Club, not because I was then much of a Liberal but because I wanted the Liberals to support Democratic Club candidates in student council elections. The first Liberal Club meeting I attended was a rowdy AGM where the old executive was replaced. At one stage, someone interjected that I didn't understand 'the Liberal grass roots'. 'They'd be the only ones you understand', I shouted back, but I think I might have been wrong, as he subsequently became a Mardi Gras organiser.

In any event, it was an early lesson in the realities of politics. The arguments in favour of student Liberals taking a more robust political stance hadn't changed, but, at least at Sydney University, the numbers certainly had. Elsewhere, though, the argument seemed to have become more compelling. Right around the country at that time, Liberal students were becoming more involved in university politics. The Australian Liberal Students Federation was formed, with Michael Kroger, Eric Abetz and Michael Yabsley prominently involved.

In the late 1970s a grand coalition of NCC, right-wing ALP, Jewish and Liberal students was working against the 'land rights for gay whales' type of activist who'd dominated student political bodies since the Vietnam War era. For a year or two, some Australian student bodies were officially campaigning for better teaching and for more marketable degrees rather than against homophobic patriarchy and American imperialism. In 1979 I became president of the Sydney University Students' Representative Council. In the campaign, I recall getting a good cheer from the students of St Johns residential college when I promised to replace the SRC's Che Guevara posters with a portrait of the Queen. There was an even bigger one for promising to install a portrait of the Pope!

A year earlier, Peter Costello had been elected president of the Monash University students association. Although not then regarded as a Liberal, he was a big part of the campaign to have the major campuses withdraw from the incorrigibly Marxist Australian Union of Students (AUS). The success of that campaign owed a great deal to public exposure of rorts inside the union. Greg Sheridan, now foreign editor of *The Australian*, and I had published our own rather lurid accounts of the 1977 AUS conference after the left-wing majority had foolishly shut out the 'capitalist press'. This was my first attempt at journalism and a good lesson in the impact of publishing.

As a conservative in 1970s campus politics, the only way to avoid being howled down was to put your arguments in writing. Unlike a speech, a letter in *Honi Soit*, the Sydney University newspaper, could not be drowned out by hecklers. I soon discovered that it was harder to take intellectual short cuts or to get away with debating tricks if your case had to stand up in print rather than just to sound plausible in a melee of voices. From the start, though, I was less interested in reporting events than in shaping them. That's hardly unusual for a politician, even a student one.

Often enough, through lack of interest or political bias, the student paper wouldn't print conservative arguments, so, even as a student politician, I became a contributor to metropolitan and even national newspapers and magazines. At first part-time while still a student and later full-time, I eventually became a journalist. What mattered to me, then and now, was the impact of ideas on events and the critical importance of a written argument in shaping people's ideas. As a journalist, I was often a frustrated politician who wanted to make decisions rather than just analyse them. Later, as a politician, I was often a frustrated journalist because decisions mostly didn't speak for themselves and had to be explained if they were to be supported. In politics, what's not reported might as well not have happened. Often, the best way to be reported was to write the report yourself. As it turned out, writing speeches on key topics, many of them later published in newspapers, has been my way of combining writing with politics.

As much, I'm sure, through my role in student politics as through academic or sporting prowess, I was chosen as a NSW Rhodes Scholar at the end of 1980. I was following in the footsteps of fellow Sydney University rugby players Michael L'Estrange (later secretary of the Department of Foreign Affairs and Trade), Roger Davis (later a senior executive at the ANZ bank), Phil Crowe (Professor of Medicine at the University of New South Wales), Malcolm Turnbull, and also his predecessor as Member for Wentworth, Peter King. After me, Sydney University rugby Rhodes Scholars included Gordon Fell (a prominent investment banker), Alec Cameron (deputy vice-chancellor of the University of New South Wales) and Ian Jackman (brother of Hugh and a Sydney silk). Under the terms of the founder's will, Rhodes Scholars are supposed to have demonstrated 'sympathy for and protection of the weak' and to have 'leadership qualities'. It was a potential leaders' scholarship, at least in those days, rather than a mainly academic one.

Someone once said that Oxford had left him 'magnificently unprepared for the long littleness of life'. For me, one legacy was a handful of friendships that have survived the tyranny of distance. I doubt that I have ever met a finer man than Paul Mankowski. It's an unusual Jesuit who turns out to be a recruiting agent for the university boxing team. A couple of extra drinks in the Eastgate Hotel finally secured my reluctant agreement one January night in 1982. After an initial training session, I was preparing my excuses when Paul presented me with a new skipping rope. This was a big investment from a man whose wardrobe was handed down from dead priests, so I didn't have the heart to quit. Within a couple of weeks, the challenge of a new and ferocious discipline naturally had me hooked. Another Oxford legacy, thanks to the tutorial system, was the ability to digest and assimilate texts and to produce to deadline a 1500-word essay. Whatever else they might be, Oxbridge undergraduate courses are superb preparation for op-ed journalism.

Oxford consolidated the intellectual formation that the Jesuits had begun but that I had mostly neglected at Sydney. Professors Alice Tay and Lauchlan Chipman's legal philosophy courses were the only ones, I'm now sorry to say, that I didn't approach in the intellectually corrosive spirit of 'tell us what we need to know to pass the exam'. These two important academic mentors persuasively insisted that it was possible to make distinctions between shades of grey on the basis not just of consequences but mankind's persistent moral instinct. They also insisted on receiving their students' own views in essays, not regurgitated quotes from the reading list.

At Oxford, I'd again been asking myself how I could best exercise leadership and, again, my thoughts had turned to the priesthood. I didn't relish more years in the classroom, was far from certain about my aptitude for parish life, and hated the prospect of lifelong celibacy. On the other hand, the notion of becoming a priest had tugged at me for years. Meeting Mankowski, a contemporary who was both the embodiment of muscular Christianity and fully acquainted with the cross tides of modern life, made me think that it might be possible to become a priest and stay 'normal'. Perhaps it was 'meant to be'. The only way I'd ever know, I concluded, was to give it a try.

Until then, the priests I'd known were nearly all natural leaders. Most of them would have excelled in any field. They tended to be sceptical about dogma and ambivalent about its leaders without being cynical about the church. The crosses they carried had not noticeably weakened their commitment to their work and message. It was a different aspect of the church, though, that I discovered at Sydney's St Patrick's seminary: by comparison with my previous experience, it often seemed highly strung and self-absorbed. The emphasis was on self-discovery rather than the heroic mission for which generations of young Catholics had been prepared to remain poor, obedient and chaste.

Even in its declining days, St Patrick's had some fine teachers: Gerry Gleeson, the Cambridge-educated philosopher whom, years later, I appointed to the health ethics committee of the National Health and Medical Research Council; David Coffey, allegedly a 'resurrection denier' but a captivating lecturer and, in my judgment, a conscientious seeker after truth; Brian Yates, who helped many students to keep their balance in an unsettling environment; and the legendary Ed Campion, who always seemed like a square peg in a round hole. Still, the fact that he stayed a priest encouraged me to think that the frustrations might be worth putting up with. Ed's comment on an essay on the Labor split was the most glowing I've ever received: 'Thank you for the pleasure this has given me', but it was rather undermined by the essay's credit result. Much that was presented as 'spiritual discernment' struck me as a form of ritual humiliation. For instance, one evening, second-year students were asked to present plasticine models that reflected their inner life. One, who was on the verge of being asked to leave, went to the front of the class, dropped his model of himself on the floor, and said 'rejected'. I had made a model aeroplane. Perhaps that meant I wanted to be somewhere else.

My restlessness during these seminary years took several forms. The then rector, Fr Grove Johnson, took an indulgent view of breaking into the tower to fly the Union Jack on St Patrick's Day. 'People have been calling to say ecumenism has taken a new turn', he observed. Substituting a rugby union match versus St Johns College for the time-honoured in-house rugby league raised a few eyebrows among seminary traditionalists. Calling for the seminary to be closed, though, in favour of training priests at the university was probably a symptom of my growing sense that I was a fish out of water.

In 1985 the new seminary rector, Fr Gerry Iverson, did not quite order me to spend the following year as a pastoral assistant in a distant parish to sort myself out, because modern churchmen are not that authoritarian. Under protest, I went to Emu Plains, but I sensed that it would work out well once the parish priest, Fr Kevin Hannan, had enquired whether I took my coffee with milk or with brandy! It was a fairly traditional parish, with enormous effort going into building Catholic schools and other good works. Kevin radiated common sense and was almost impossible to surprise, even when I rang him at 3 a.m. from somewhere in the Blue Mountains, having fallen asleep on the train home after a rugby dinner, wanting him to drive through the snow to collect me. The parish and its parishioners were a fine illustration of how a sense of higher purpose can infuse ordinary life in ways that help to bring out the good in people. Sharing their life helped me to appreciate better that you certainly didn't have to be a priest to do God's work.

At about this time, my yearning for the wider world was being fanned (perhaps inadvertently) by the Catholic Labor stalwart Johno Johnson, who on a number of occasions had invited me to dinners with NSW government ministers in the president's dining room of the NSW parliament. Back at the seminary again after my 'pastoral' year, looking for a diversion on a sleepy afternoon, I phoned a university rugby friend only to be told that a get-together the following week would have to be postponed because he was going to London to sign a multi-billion-dollar contract. That was the moment I irrevocably concluded that a 29-year-old former Rhodes Scholar writing 500-word essays in the company of uncertain youths and middle-aged nuns was not making the most of his life.

Looking back, there were three reasons I would not have made a very good priest. The living Jesus of Christian faith was only a second-hand presence in my life. I knew his friends, so to speak, who impressed me immensely, but I wasn't 'naturally devout', at least in the ways necessary to sustain life as a priest. Not consoled by heartfelt prayer, I couldn't imagine being celibate for the rest of my life. Finally, I was far from confident that I had the patience to be effective in a parish. I craved more excitement than the priesthood seemed to offer, notwithstanding, as I was later to discover, the 'poverty, chastity and obedience' dimension that exists in most lives.

While still at St Patrick's, I'd had a few months of part-time journalism on *The Catholic Weekly*. This ceased because, as I was told, the then archbishop, Cardinal Clancy, didn't especially like being lectured to by a seminarian in his own newspaper. Instead, especially during my seminary vacations, I wrote articles for *The Bulletin*, including a long account of the Pope's 1986 visit to Australia. The seminary authorities' unease at my interest in writing was another factor in my slow discovery that I wasn't meant to be a priest.

So, early in 1987, I finally moved from being an occasional contributor to newspapers and magazines into full-time journalism. The late 1980s was an era of structural reform in business. One day, Australian Consolidated Press sacked the entire photography department, including people with over thirty years' service to the company. I moved the motion to strike. Ultimately, the journalists produced a weekly magazine for three days' pay, while the photographers subsequently earned considerably more as freelancers than as employees.

After twelve months at *The Bulletin*, I had a stint managing a concrete-batching plant courtesy of Sir Tristan Antico, a prominent member of the wider Jesuit network, who was good enough to accommodate my interest in a job that could not be dismissed as 'ivory tower'. One afternoon, after the plant operator had gone home, several truckloads of sand and aggregate arrived to beat a planned quarry strike. Once I'd worked out how to start the conveyor belts, they were able to dump their loads. At 5.30 a.m. the next day, the dispatcher called me at home to warn that this initiative meant that my plant had been declared 'black'. The union organiser said that it was 'more than his job was worth' to let the company get away with it. I quickly worked out that this was a problem that I had to fix on my own and that grovelling was the only way. After a long dressing-down, the organiser gave me the 'final warning' that I'd suggested might justify lifting the ban. I'd learned an important lesson, though: that you have to engage people before you can give them orders. About a month later, after I'd taken to spending an hour each day in the plant crib room, the dispatcher gave me standing permission to turn on the conveyor belts. Within six months, we were digging out slurry pits together.

By then I was married with a baby on the way. For a time, my interest in politics actually helped the family. I went back to journalism, as a leader writer at *The Australian*, because it meant higher pay. After a year there, again on a better offer, this time brokered by the then former leader, John Howard, I became press secretary (and later political adviser) to the then opposition leader, John Hewson.

Hewson and I had our differences, but I owe him a lot. He asked me to be the principal draftsman of the main Fightback! document, which meant that I had to master the arguments for the policies that largely shaped Australia over the next decade and a half. Hewson might have failed as a political leader, but, as the Keating and Howard Governments proceeded to implement most of his agenda, he turned out to be one of Australia's most influential policy makers. Because he didn't like speaking from the scripts that I had often drafted for him, I used to lament that I had become the unsung author of some of the great undelivered political orations. Re-reading some of Hewson's speeches for this book, I can see that the work wasn't wholly wasted. In any event, writing for the spike is a speech writer's lot. Learning about politics from the inside and dealing with the press gallery as a staffer rather than a colleague certainly helped in my next role as executive director of Australians for Constitutional Monarchy.

In between jobs in April 1993, while I was an unemployed ex-staffer wondering how to pay the mortgage, Johno Johnson launched his final recruitment drive. I should return to my 'true home', he said.

I responded that I'd never left the church. 'Not that one', he said, 'the Labor Party'. At length, I explained that I was indeed dismayed by the Liberals' post-election manoeuvring but added that I was even more appalled by Paul Keating's attack on the monarchy. 'Comrade, there is no hope for you', said the Labor legend, hanging up the phone. A few months later, I bumped into Johno while going into the NSW parliament for a monarchists' lunch. 'If you'd accepted my advice, you'd be a member of this place by now', he said. It was good-natured teasing from a fine man who is a friend to this day. Neither of us was to know that within a few more months I'd be a Liberal MP in Canberra.

I wasn't expected to win the pre-selection for Warringah, a safe-ish seat that the long-serving sitting member vacated in January 1994. A good speech, though, enabled me to 'come through the middle' of a crowded field. The notes for that speech included what were to become some recurrent themes:

> All my life, I have tried to stand up for the causes I believed in … As a journalist, I never began an article with the assumption that there was something fundamentally wrong with our country and I tried to find the good in the people and institutions I covered … In the Leader of the Opposition's office, I tried to be a reminder that politics is about inspiration as much as policy and that we have to like people as well as lecture to them—to reach out to them and give them hope in our country and in themselves …
>
> I'm a Liberal because I believe that government's role is to give people a hand up, not a handout. I believe in limited government and unlimited opportunity, because for getting things done free enterprise beats red tape every time … I'm a Liberal because our party has always stood for the decent, the humane and usually for the practical too … We know that without honesty there is no trust and without trust there is no fairness and without fairness civil society cannot long survive.

> We should give ourselves more credit for our achievements. It was Bob Menzies and not John Curtin who first called Asia our Near North. It was Bob Menzies and not Paul Keating who redirected our trade to Asia in the 1960s … It was Harold Holt and not Gough Whitlam who ended the White Australia policy and it was John Howard [as treasurer in the Fraser Government] and not Bob Hawke who began financial deregulation …
>
> Australia's new poor are families with children … It's time that we looked seriously at a tax system which recognises people's responsibilities and not just their incomes … Life in Warringah is great, until you need to go somewhere. I know transport is a state issue, but that wouldn't stop me from pressing the state government to support a solution and, if needs be, seeking federal government help too …
>
> In the end, politics is about values as much as policies. The only lasting solution to unemployment is self-reliance and the best cure for out-of-control welfare spending is keeping families together. If there is one contribution that I would most like to make to our national life it would be stop knocking our country … To this end, I set out to defend the constitution of our country … and to make a cause that was all but finished intellectually respectable again. And that cause, the monarchy, happened to be the first plank of the foundation platform of the Liberal Party … [Now I want] to work for an even better cause: reclaiming our political culture and helping Australia to achieve the greatness that we all know is within our grasp …

Fifteen years later, I am still talking about what it means to be a Liberal, the financial predicament of families with children, the dysfunctional federation and, above all, how to nurture a better Australia by building on our strengths. I still think that the job of government is to respond intelligently to the problems of the day and, in so doing, to help our country to reflect better its best values. I'm comfortable on the Liberal Party's more conservative wing because conservatism is a pragmatic, eclectic creed, above all respectful of what's stood the test of time. As John Howard once quipped, 'a conservative is someone who doesn't think he's morally superior to his grandfather'.

In the meantime, I've been a backbencher in opposition, a parliamentary secretary, a junior minister, Minister for Employment and Workplace Relations, Minister for Health, and Leader of the House of Representatives as well as, currently, Shadow Minister for Families, Housing, Community Services and Indigenous Affairs. Perhaps my most significant contribution to the Howard Government, though, was frequent scripted speeches that sought to explain and justify the values behind its policies. Often enough, I was the designated 'attack dog' in the media on difficult issues where the prime minister wanted back-up. I didn't always relish that role, but someone has to do it. Political parties, no less than rugby teams, need some hard men.

Since the election, I've been pondering the lessons in the term of the former government: why did it succeed and why did it eventually fail; what are the Liberal Party's best values and how can they be translated into policy; and what aspects of Australia should we be trying to change or to reinforce? That's what the rest of this book is about.

2 A Tale of Two Governments

One afternoon in August 2007, John Howard, Peter Costello and I met to discuss hospital policy. For most of my time as health minister, public hospitals had been a contentious issue inside the government. Back in February 2004, at a conference in Sydney, Premier Bob Carr had blamed NSW public hospital problems on the lack of Commonwealth government funding. In response, I had said that if the state government was incapable of running public hospitals, it should surrender that responsibility to the Commonwealth. From that time on, it was my consistent position that having responsibility for funding public hospitals but no authority whatsoever over how they were run was a very unsatisfactory arrangement for the Commonwealth government.

On several subsequent occasions, I'd publicly expressed this view, sometimes to the prime minister's irritation. Eventually, the Howard Government concluded that, as a condition of receiving increased funding under the next round of Health Care Agreements, the states would have to run public hospitals in the way the Commonwealth would if it actually had the responsibility for doing so. As I subsequently explained, the intention was to 'back seat drive' public hospital management by including impossible-to-fudge conditions in the next set of agreements.[1] The states would have to establish local boards to appoint CEOs with real authority over hospital budgets. In June 2007, when the Tasmanian government moved to downgrade the Mersey hospital near Devonport, the prime minister announced a Commonwealth takeover of this particular hospital with the establishment of a local board to run it.

On the day before that meeting, the leader of the opposition had trumped these initiatives, declaring that a Labor government would work with the states to improve public hospital standards. Further, in the event that these did not improve within 18 months, a Labor government would seek to take over and run the states' public hospital systems. There was no detail, of course, but it was a dramatic way to let voters know that federal Labor took public hospital problems seriously.

Bold moves make big headlines. Compared with a Commonwealth government takeover, the establishment of local boards to run public hospitals looked like a second-order change. Even though a Commonwealth takeover that did not involve devolution to local control would just have replaced one lot of bureaucrats with another, 'Commonwealth takeover' sounds more impressive than 'new management structures'. In a political climate where everything that one side did was perceived as 'poll-driven desperation' and everything the other did seemed a breath of fresh air, the Howard initiative didn't stand a chance.

The meeting in the prime minister's Sydney office was to consider raising the stakes: should the government reverse its previous position and seek to end the interminable blame shifting by taking over all public hospitals immediately after the election, if necessary through changing the constitution? The discussion went backwards and forwards for well over an hour. Various other options were canvassed: taking over more hospitals that the states were running down to show how they might be run better; using the Health Care Agreements to force the states to contract out public hospital services; and directly funding hospitals to provide a particular quantum of free services to public patients; in addition to the 'mega' option of a full Commonwealth government takeover.

As usual with policy debates inside the Howard Government, the discussion was animated but civil. No one pulled rank. No one set out to be the custodian of ideological purity. In the end, though, no decision was taken, because there was no course of action upon which all three of us could agree. An immediate Commonwealth takeover might have looked like responding to the other side. As well, it would have provoked the Liberal Party's 'anti-centralism' brigade, even though it was the states that had run hospitals from head office through giant unwieldy bureaucracies. At that stage in the political cycle, anything dramatic would have been cast as an admission of past failure.

The truth was that the Howard Government had become a prisoner of its record, as all long-lived governments eventually do. We couldn't make a decisive break with the past eleven years because to do so would be to repudiate what we'd previously done. As a result, among much else detrimental to our political fortunes, Labor maintained its clear Newspoll lead as the party 'best placed to handle health and Medicare'. The government continued to take hits for political problems that weren't its fault but which it had no way to fix. For me, this was the most telling illustration of the political senescence to which all long-term governments are prone. It wasn't that the government was bereft of ideas or of the energy to implement them. It was more that almost nothing could be done that didn't prompt people to think that it should have been done sooner.

In some respects, 2007 had been a vintage year for innovative government policy: the $10 billion Murray–Darling initiative had the potential to end decades of interstate squabbling over water; polls rated that year's budget the best ever; the government offered to half-fund all unmet need for disability accommodation provided that the states could find the rest of the money; finally, the intervention in the Northern Territory's remote townships was a once-in-a-generation policy watershed. All these measures were widely welcomed, but none seemed to make the slightest difference to the government's political standing. It had simply run out of goodwill from the electorate.

The Liberal Party had misinterpreted the 2004 election result as a vote of confidence in John Howard and of no confidence in Labor.

In fact, it reflected the electorate's preference for proven performance over risky experiment. There's every chance that the 2007 result will also be misinterpreted as a fundamental rejection of Liberal policy (at least as practised by John Howard) and an embrace of the ALP itself. Fundamentally, it was time that beat John Howard, not Labor. Of course, the government's mistakes, the ACTU's unprecedented ad campaign, and Labor's political cleverness in choosing an unthreatening new leader all helped. The bottom line, though, is that voters had decided that it was time for a change. They didn't vote against Howard or for Rudd so much as for something new.

In a sense, the former government was a victim of its own success. As reforms were progressively implemented, unemployment fell, and incomes and wealth grew, voters inevitably began to take good times for granted. People with no memories of strikes weren't scared of unions. People with no experience of unemployment didn't see why further economic reform was necessary. As the Commonwealth government progressively tackled the issues that were its responsibility, voters increasingly expected it to address problems that were the responsibilities of the states. Why couldn't a government that had cut taxes and repaid all Commonwealth debt do something about infrastructure? Why couldn't the massive surplus be invested in better public schools and hospitals? Paradoxically, federal Labor was the political beneficiary of the failures of the state Labor governments, which it cleverly managed to pin on alleged Howard Government neglect.

As someone once said, in politics, friends come and go, but enemies accumulate. Nearly every decision has the potential to leave someone with a grievance, even if it's only 'why didn't I get more?' Often, success just breeds higher expectations. As nearly every political leader sooner or later discovers, the electorate can be a fickle mistress.

There were mistakes, too, but none of them would have been as politically damaging if the years had not entirely eroded the electorate's readiness to give the incumbent any benefit of the doubt. The second wave of industrial relations reform, Work Choices, was a catastrophic political blunder because it undermined the Howard battlers' faith in the Prime Minister's goodwill. Although there had long been a distinct and highly articulate group of inveterate Howard haters, these had never been politically decisive, as the election results demonstrated in 2001 and 2004, when the 'republic, reconciliation and refugees' lobby was at its most morally indignant. There's no reason to think that boat people, the war in Iraq or the Guantanamo detainee David Hicks were any more electorally significant in the 2007 election than they had been in the previous one. With Howard, it was keeping the support of the 'blue collar conservatives', not the 'doctors' wives', that had always made the difference between winning and losing.

It's often noted that Howard had lost what Judith Brett has called the 'moral middle class' over asylum seekers and climate change. There's little doubt that some Liberal voters were uneasy about the government's positions on these issues. Those that were going to change their votes on them, though, almost certainly would have done so prior to the 2007 poll.

Howard's concern not to 'waste' the Senate majority unexpectedly obtained in 2004 was understandable, but a better approach would have been to bundle up previously rejected workplace legislation rather than to have gone further and abolished the 'no disadvantage' test. Even though Work Choices coincided with the fastest jobs growth in Australia's history and examples of exploitation usually turned out to be not quite what they seemed, an impression was created that the government no longer cared about vulnerable workers. The conservative working people who had loathed Paul Keating, taken the Goods and Services Tax on trust, cheered Work for the Dole, and supported the war on terror didn't reject John Howard himself over Work Choices (his personal popularity remained at about 50 per cent), but they certainly rejected his government.

In the aftermath of defeat, there's always speculation about what might have been. A certain amount of 'crying over spilt milk' may be hard to avoid if the lessons of defeat are to be absorbed. Peter Costello remains understandably disappointed that he was denied the chance to remake the government. Far from being the catalyst for a leadership change, Ian McLachlan's 2006 revelation of a leadership 'deal' that was supposed to have delivered the prime ministership to Costello back in 2000 may have ended up reinforcing doubts about how hard the treasurer would fight for the top job. The revelation also made it much harder for Howard to quit. Perversely, given McLachlan's belief that Costello had the best chance of winning the election, 'Walletgate' brought matters to a head in a way that all but guaranteed Howard would fight the next election. At least for a time, even the former treasurer's strongest supporters concluded that keeping Howard was the government's best bet.

It's possible that Costello could have managed renewal in office after the year-out-from-an-election handover that Howard had been contemplating. On the other hand, the treasurer and the prime minister had been a very close political partnership for a very long time. Politically effective policy innovation would have been almost as hard for a prime minister Costello as it was for Prime Minister Howard. It would have been much harder for Costello to walk away from unpopular policies than it was (say) for the relatively unknown Premier Morris Iemma to distance himself from the Carr legacy. It would have been much harder for Costello to beat a political chameleon like Kevin Rudd than it had been for Paul Keating to beat John Hewson, who was too politically honest for his own good. There have been relatively successful transitions from long-term leaders: from Menzies to Holt, for instance, and from Bolte to Hamer. This might have been how it worked out had the leadership passed from Howard to Costello in the government's fourth term. On the other hand, there have been plenty of unsuccessful transitions, too, such as from Askin to Lewis and then Willis, and from Bolte to Thompson. As things have worked out, no one will ever know.

With 20-20 hindsight, it's easy to conclude that 'Howard stayed too long'. A political party in trouble is always tempted to try anything but the status quo. What's often forgotten is the danger that the alternative could be worse. I always thought that Peter Costello was by far the government's most formidable politician after Howard. Outstanding though he was, however, I never thought that a government without Howard would be stronger than one with him.

The 'might have beens' of APEC (Asia Pacific Economic Community) week in Sydney in September 2007 have already been pored over to excess. In fairness to readers, though, here is my part in the tremor of doubt that collectively ran through the cabinet. On the Wednesday, the influential columnist Janet Albrechtsen addressed a lunch for the Liberal Party's Forestville branch in my electorate. She drew me aside to say that she intended to write in her Friday column that Howard should go, because the polls showed that he couldn't win the election due in two months, but she wanted to let him know that this was coming. My response was that Howard remained the best leader and the best electoral asset we had. It was clear, when I spoke to Howard himself straight after the lunch, that he was under no illusions about our prospects. The only question that mattered was could Peter Costello do better?

Howard said that he'd been canvassing this issue for some time with foreign minister Alexander Downer, had authorised Downer to take soundings and would be happy for me to do so also. I then spoke to Senate leader Nick Minchin, who said that he'd thought we should have changed leaders at about the time of the government's tenth anniversary but that it would be madness to change now. I called Costello, who also thought that it was too late to win the election but that, if the prime minister stood aside, of course he'd take the job and do his best. Finally, I spoke to Downer, who thought that we couldn't win with Howard but just might win with Costello and probably should risk the change. I subsequently asked two friends, one usually a Liberal voter, the other not, plus a family member, all of whom said that changing the leader now would look like panic and would make the inevitable defeat much worse. I called Howard to let him know that this was my considered view. My mistake was not calling Downer, who had gained the impression that I was at least open to change. This was fair enough as, in our conversation, I had been trying to keep an open mind, but it didn't help when Downer met with more than half the cabinet the following night.

Of course, the Downer meeting leaked, reinforcing the impression of a government gripped by fear and division. In a dire situation, why shouldn't the prime minister have asked his colleagues whether they would prefer to take their chances with someone else and why shouldn't cabinet members have had an all-options-on-the-table discussion? The whole exercise, though, just demonstrated that when nothing is going right everything turns out for the worse.

Once the federal Labor Party had united behind a non-threatening new leader, the government was inevitably going to suffer from the 'it's time' factor. A big fifth-term agenda, such as tackling the dysfunctional federation, would have been worthy of a great reforming prime minister, but even that probably would not have staved off defeat. Howard had too much integrity to copy Premiers Carr, Peter Beattie and Steve Bracks who quit after promising to serve a full term. That meant voting for Howard but electing Costello, which was a 'big ask' of voters.

The challenge is to learn from what the former government did wrong in its final term but not to exaggerate its mistakes or be paralysed by them. It's to learn from what the then opposition did right but not to be intimidated by it. Governments deserve to be judged on what they did as well as on how they lost. A measure of the former government's success is the once-contentious policies that the new government said it would keep. The Rudd Government has abolished Work Choices but has kept much of its substance: secret ballots before strikes, restrictions on what awards can cover, and (at least for a time) forms of individual statutory contracts. The new government has ratified the Kyoto climate change agreement but has largely adopted the Howard Government's proposed emissions trading scheme as its way to reduce carbon dioxide emissions. It has apologised for past wrongs to Aboriginal people but has largely maintained the emergency intervention in the Northern Territory. Troops have been withdrawn from the anti-terrorist campaign in Iraq, but there's been no reduced commitment to the war in Afghanistan. Even the Howard Government's school chaplaincy program has been maintained, although counsellors can be substituted where no suitable chaplain is available. The ultimate tribute to the former government is the extent to which its successor has felt the need to copy it.

In very significant ways, the Howard Government changed the country for the better. Australia's economic performance between 1996 and 2007 already seems like a lost golden age. Strong international markets played their part, but so did outstandingly good management, as demonstrated by Australia's successful avoidance of the Asian slowdown in the late 1990s and the tech-wreck recession after 2000. Not for nothing was Australia seen as the world's stellar economy. Between 1996 and 2006, while the US economy grew by 3.2 per cent a year, that of the United Kingdom by 2.8 per cent and that of the OECD by 2.7 per cent, Australia's economic growth averaged 3.6 per cent a year. Over the life of the Howard Government, Australia's Index of Economic Freedom ranking went from tenth to fourth. Australia's UN Human Development Index ranking went from fifteenth to third.

Unemployment averaged 8.5 per cent under the Hawke and Keating Governments but 6.3 per cent under the Howard Government. Real average weekly earnings rose by just 0.1 per cent under the former Labor government but by 24.4 per cent under its successor. Labour-force participation averaged 62.3 per cent between 1983 and 1996 but 63.6 per cent between 1996 and 2007. Housing interest rates averaged 12.75 per cent under Labor but 7.26 per cent under the coalition. Net Commonwealth debt, which reached $96 billion under Labor, disappeared under the coalition. Inflation averaged 5.5 per cent under Labor but just 2.5 per cent under the coalition.

The frequent claim that the former government created a strong economy at the expense of a fair society is just wrong. The National Centre for Social and Economic Modelling has shown that, during the Howard years, the poorest 10 per cent of the population got richer at about the same rate as the richest 10 per cent. The group that did best was actually middle-income families with children—Kevin Rudd's 'working families'. As well, the number of people who had been unemployed for two years or more dropped from 115,000 to just 36,000.

It seems that the former government measured up on values indicators too. As the *Sydney Morning Herald* journalist Peter Hartcher has pointed out, Australians' charitable giving increased by 88 per cent between 1997 and 2004—after inflation an average annual growth of 8.3 per cent, more than double the growth in GDP. As well, the proportion of Australians donating their time to a non-profit organisation rose from 24 per cent to 41 per cent between 1995 and 2005. So much for Howard turning Australians into 'greed is good' capitalists!

The new government has accused its predecessor of just surfing the China boom. In fact, catching economic waves takes some skill. In the '70s and '80s, Brazil developed its iron ore industry largely on the back of Australia's unreliability as a supplier. In the March quarter of 1996, there were 7762 days lost per 1000 workers due to industrial action in the resources sector. In the September quarter of 2007, no days were lost to strikes in the non-coal mining sector and just 1.5 days were lost per 1000 workers in coal. In November last year, as the unions flexed their muscles under the new government, the Pilbara iron ore region had its first rail strike in more than twelve years. In 1995–96 there were 800,000 working days lost through strikes. This had dropped to under 100,000 by 2006–07 (the lowest since 1913, when records were first kept) but almost doubled in 2007–08, with all the increase taking place after the election of the Rudd Government.

The claim that the long boom owed everything to China and nothing to the Howard Government's reforms is almost laughably partisan. As former Treasury head John Stone has observed:

> A rise of almost one-third in real GDP per head over the short space of twelve years is so impressive in its own right as not to require any further egging of that pudding via the terms of trade enhancement of it. To change the culinary metaphor, that was mere icing—albeit very sweet icing—on the cake.[2]

It's not entirely surprising that Kevin Rudd should, depending on his audience, dismiss the impact of the Howard reforms because, in social democrat guise, he dismisses the Hawke–Keating reforms too. The Howard Government's GST reforms addressed the problem that the Hawke Government tried to fix but couldn't with its Option C (a broad-based retail sales tax). The Howard Government's first round of workplace reform extended the enterprise bargaining initiatives first introduced by the Keating Government in 1993. Workplace relations minister Peter Reith's waterfront reforms achieved what was said to be impossible after the maritime unions had successfully sabotaged the Hawke Government's efforts. Peter Costello's 1996 budget cuts were a more robust version of former finance minister Peter Walsh's cuts in the mid-1980s. The thirty years of 'neo-liberalism' that Rudd rejects in his latest, February 2009, essay for *The Monthly* includes all the economic reforms of his Labor predecessors since Gough Whitlam.

A key difference between the Howard reforms and those of the Hawke and Keating Governments is that Howard's were carried out in the teeth of ferocious political opposition from the Labor Party, which swiftly rejected in opposition the economic responsibility it had often displayed in government. From the time of the waterfront dispute almost until he left parliament, Peter Reith needed round-the-clock protection. For much of this period, he was unable to live in his family home. Costello's reductions to the budget estimates, especially his non-renewal of the Keating Government's dental subsidy and reduction in the anticipated rate of growth of Commonwealth hospital spending, were still being thrown at him and at the government eleven years later. Even though Labor did not oppose them, Howard's gun-control laws took considerable courage, as the number of death threats that police took seriously demonstrated.

Howard turned out to be the great boundary buster of Australian politics. In tax, workplace relations, welfare, immigration, trade, Indigenous affairs and foreign policy, he made the politically impossible achievable. Except for the public service, airlines, car manufacturing and commercial construction, in the day-to-day running of business unions became almost irrelevant. While constantly criticising its implementation, Labor ended up backing the government's treatment of unauthorised arrivals and special laws to make it harder for illegal entrants to stay. The Labor Party opposed Work for the Dole when it was first introduced but ended up supporting it (albeit without real conviction), as well as work interviews for supporting parents, and tougher tests for people seeking the disability support pension. Even though it overturned a generation of welfarist thinking (and Labor government practice), Labor more or less supported the NT intervention.

Perhaps most significantly, under Howard, for the first time, Australia became an international power in its own right. The liberation of East Timor and the peace-keeping missions to the failing states of the Pacific were wholly Australian initiatives. Far from being America's 'deputy sheriff' (a journalist's tag unfairly pinned on the former prime minister), Australia ran a kind of neighbourhood watch scheme in support of Western values. The free trade agreement with the United States, now taken for granted, was a historic coup significantly integrating Australia into the world's strongest economy.

Frustrations notwithstanding, Peter Costello has said that Howard has a claim to be considered 'Australia's greatest prime minister' with only the 'possible exception' of Sir Robert Menzies.[3] John Stone, who often attacked the former prime minister for being, at best, a Fabian conservative, concluded that, in the history of the anglosphere, his niche will rank 'alongside the places of Margaret Thatcher and Ronald Reagan in Britain and the United States. While each of those outstanding leaders had qualities different from Howard's, each, like him, came to office at what, looking back, we now see to have been turning points in their nations' histories'.[4]

What's often now forgotten is the sense of inadequacy verging on failure that haunted Australia for much of the period between Whitlam and Howard. In economic terms, the Menzies-era pride that we were a rich country getting richer gave way to the fear that we were a rich country becoming poorer. Underlying much of the argument for multiculturalism, reconciliation and republicanism was nagging doubt about Australia's legitimacy as a country. Howard's greatest single achievement was to banish this doubt. His faith in Australia restored that of millions. Even those who, deep down, still found their country an embarrassment were able to blame its deficiencies on the prime minister rather than on the Australian people.

Imitation is, of course, the greatest compliment of all. After Kevin Rudd became leader, the Labor Party's public position largely changed from being an opposition to an echo. Unlike his predecessors, who had emphasised how different they would be, Rudd was almost unique as an opposition leader in fighting an election promising to keep most of the government's key policies rather than to change them. Inevitably, the longer the Rudd Government lasts, the more its predecessor's programs will be watered down and its values subverted. Labor frontbencher Peter Garrett's election-eve prediction that 'we'll change it all once we're in government' will largely come to pass. Still, much will endure as a permanent tribute to the Howard Government and, provided people keep their heads, an inspiration to Liberals despondent about their political prospects.

Winning the next election won't be easy but it's certainly possible. Provided the opposition remains credible, there's little reason to be sure that the Rudd Government will be in a politically strong position when the next election is due in late 2010. The government's poll ratings are still high, but that's understandable under the circumstances. People don't swiftly turn on those they've just chosen to lead the country, especially when there's no new need for them to choose and when each day, at least until the money dries up, there's a new act of 'decisive leadership'. In its only direct electoral test, last year's Gippsland by-election, there was, in fact, a 6 per cent swing against the Rudd Government.

In two critical respects, the new government already suffers by comparison to its predecessor: first, it lacks any clear rationale, or narrative, for the blizzard of announcements and almost manic activity in which it's engaged; and second, its leader is not a well-formed political personality whose acts seem to be considered expressions of consistent convictions.

Good polls give politicians confidence but aren't the real measure of a government's quality. For instance, the consistent poll leads of the NSW Labor government (at least until its fourth term) owed much more to news management than to substance. The Rudd Government's announcement strategy is a direct lift from NSW Labor, which has perfected the media spin satirised in the ABC's *Hollowmen* TV series. Burying a failed policy by announcing an even bigger one has become a standard Rudd Government tactic. The prime minister and his colleagues' Orwellian references to a 'temporary' deficit (even though it will last at least for seven years), 'protecting jobs' (even though unemployment is tipped to exceed one million by 2011) and 'decisive action' (even though most of what's proposed won't happen for years) is obviously open to parody. Still, they must think that this kind of manipulation works. Sooner or later the public will work out that making an announcement is not the same as making a difference but, like Premier Carr, Prime Minister Rudd probably thinks that he'll be long gone by then. Over the past fifteen years, for instance, the NSW government has announced $28 billion worth of rail projects alone that have turned out to be pie in the sky.[5] In the same vein, there's little likelihood that the Rudd Government's $43 billion initiative to provide broadband to 90 per cent of households (replacing its failed $4.9 billion election initiative to provide broadband to 98 per cent of households) will ever be delivered.

A more difficult issue for the government to 'spin away' will be the likely failure of its much-hyped schools initiatives. There are already widespread reports that stimulus package money is being wasted because, under state government rules, schools have to accept inflated 'preferred tenderer' bids for new infrastructure. Even if the government manages to deliver its 'education revolution' computers to schools, many of them will stay in boxes because there aren't sufficient trained teachers or enough new software packages to make unwrapping them worthwhile. Justifying stimulus measures that don't stave off a recession but do create massive debt will challenge even this government's PR skills.

As the government implicitly acknowledged once the financial meltdown became apparent in September last year, it had inherited an economy that was the envy of other countries. Its belated assertions about the fundamental strength of the Australian economy contradicted its initial complaints about the mess it had been handed. Trying to discredit its predecessor, both Prime Minister Rudd and Treasurer Wayne Swan had so talked up the inflation 'monster', allegedly created by Howard and Costello, that the Reserve Bank felt the need to raise interest rates twice after the election.

It turned out that this was precisely the wrong time to be dampening the economy. In October last year there was the first recession-busting stimulus package: $10.4 billion worth of pre-Christmas give-aways for pensioners, and families with children. Later, there was the $42 billion stimulus package, with the lion's share of funding for school halls, housing-commission estates and home insulation. In principle, these were worthy causes. In practice, they were very hard to justify as the highest spending priorities when money was becoming tight.

To every bad economic indicator, the government's response seemed to be a new spending announcement. On top of two rounds of cash handouts and the broadband rollout, there was an extra $15 billion in COAG initiatives, $2 billion towards the 'Ruddbank' to prop up commercial property prices and an extra $3 billion for the car industry. In under twelve months, a projected $22 billion budget surplus for 2008–09 turned into a $32 billion budget deficit. It was hard to discern any plausible rationale for tackling a debt-driven recession with yet more debt except the political imperative to be seen to be doing something in the face of a looming crisis.

Perhaps one of the clearest examples of the government 'making it up as it went along' was the bank deposit guarantee. The government had been planning only to guarantee deposits up to $20,000 but then made it an unlimited, free guarantee to avoid the appearance of responding to the new opposition leader, Malcolm Turnbull, who had earlier said that the guarantee should cover deposits up to at least $100,000. This open-ended guarantee on bank deposits soon produced a run on non-banks, with some 250,000 retirees losing access to $25 billion in savings. Later, even the Labor states claimed that the bank guarantee had made it impossible for them to borrow except at considerably higher cost.

Prime Minister Rudd's economic self-descriptions have evolved from 'old-fashioned Christian socialist' (while he was establishing his credentials inside the ALP) to 'economic conservative' (up against John Howard) to 'social democrat' (justifying his big-spending response to the world recession). It's possible that these were ploys reflecting his reading of the political need of the moment, but it's more likely that he has few real convictions or little deep economic insight. It's true that better economists than the prime minister have succumbed to half-baked Keynesianism in response to the global financial crisis. What's invariably been forgotten, in the rush to emulate it, is that the New Deal did not end the Great Depression in America. In 1929, US unemployment was 3.2 per cent. It was 19 per cent ten years later. By contrast, in both Australia and Britain, which had concentrated on keeping debt under control, by 1938 unemployment had returned to pre-slump figures.[6]

Then there's the new prime minister's personal style. So far, he's been happy to claim responsibility for anything that's thought to be popular. Everything that people might not like, though, is due to the global financial crisis, or the former government is really to blame. There's little evidence of a Bob Hawke–like capacity to turn old-fashioned socialists into reluctant reformers through force of personality and weight of argument. Last October's notorious leaked phone call had a savvy Prime Minister Rudd browbeating an ignorant President Bush. There's something unsettling about an Australian prime minister who needs to big-note himself by appearing to 'verbal' the American president.

Rudd dominates the government, but his ubiquity owes as much to reluctance to delegate as to the increasingly 'presidential' way in which politics is reported. Except for Deputy Prime Minister Julia Gillard, it's not an Obama-like 'cabinet of rivals'. Key economic decisions, such as the broadband rollout, are reportedly taken by a committee of Rudd, Gillard, Treasurer Wayne Swan and finance minister Lindsay Tanner, not by cabinet. Swan is hard-working and earnest but lacks authority. Tanner presents well but, if recent decisions are a guide, he is the token economic conservative, who has either been rolled by his colleagues or reverted to his original socialism. Gillard, the architect of Medicare Gold and computers in boxes, has yet to demonstrate much ability to carry through a program but is by far the government's most convincing advocate. Unlike other ministers, she rarely sounds as though she's reading from a public servant's autocue.

Privately, Rudd's more experienced colleagues have misgivings about their leader. As Mark Latham likes to remind people, Rudd lacks close friends or staunch allies to rely on when his popularity finally fades. He could soon find himself under pressure from his ambitious deputy, who seems more authentic, even to people who mistrust her hard-left antecedents and question what kind of prime minister she would make.

So far, the government has been better at identifying issues of concern than doing much about them. Take, for instance, its much-hyped commitment to tackle truancy. This was a classic illustration of government-by-headline. For several days in August last year, the government's 'new, national anti-truancy measures' were a big political story following a front-page splash in *The Daily Telegraph*. In fact, it was merely the re-announcement of a modest budget measure: to trial welfare *suspension* at eight schools with 3300 pupils. In turn, this was a refinement of a previously announced trial (at the same eight sites) *quarantining* the welfare payments of truants' parents to the necessities of life. This trial had been based on 2007 Howard Government legislation (as part of the NT intervention), which had first ended welfare recipients' automatic entitlement to cash. The announcement's fine print actually revealed that a trial supposed, at budget time last year, to start in the second half of 2008 had in fact been put back to the first half of 2009.

For a man who campaigned as Howard-lite, once in office, Kevin Rudd's approach contrasted sharply with that of his predecessor. Prior to becoming prime minister, Howard had declared his intention to 'under-promise but over-deliver'. In its first year, the Howard Government cut almost 1 per cent of GDP from government spending, banned semi-automatic weapons and passed its first round of workplace relations legislation. Prime Minister Howard was overseas for just nineteen days in his first year. In its first year, the Rudd Government launched more than 160 reviews, committees and inquiries (of which the 2020 summit, the Henry review of tax and the Harmer review of pensions were merely the most notable). Prime Minister Rudd was overseas for fifty-nine of his first 365 days in office, including for several weeks in the lead-up to the government's first budget.

The longer the Rudd Government lasts, the more favourably the Howard Government is likely to be remembered. In part, this will be a consequence of more difficult economic times. Mostly, though, it will be a function of the two governments' very different ways of going about their business. Prime Minister Rudd is a micromanager, especially of decisions likely to generate media coverage. Because he can't admit to mistakes, relatively trivial decisions are overanalysed and researched to death. In turn, this means that some very big decisions, such as the one to provide an unlimited, free guarantee of all bank deposits, are taken 'on the fly', with serious unintended consequences.

A more basic problem, though, is that Rudd became prime minister without a developed body of thought to provide a starting point for policy and decision-making. His most considered public statements, prior to becoming prime minister, were two essays for *The Monthly*, in October and November 2006. The first, 'Faith in Politics', was a pitch for the religious vote on the basis that social justice was at the heart of Christianity. The second, 'Howard's Brutopia', claimed that the former prime minister was a free-market ideologue who had destroyed social justice (notwithstanding that his government had helped to deliver more jobs, higher pay and much greater wealth). These two articles certainly helped to position Rudd for his assault on the Labor leadership but hardly constituted sustained policy analysis.

The Labor Party, in opposition, had been largely incapable of resolving the split between market-oriented managerialists (such as Lindsay Tanner and resources minister Martin Ferguson) and sentimental socialists (such as industry minister Kim Carr and Senate firebrand Doug Cameron), so it went into the 2007 election with a few slogans and the 'it's time' factor rather than serious, properly developed alternative policy. It's most elaborate policy, Forward with Fairness, had begun as an ACTU wish list (with bargaining fees for non-union members and more-or-less mandatory union bargaining at workplaces with union members) but morphed, under employer pressure, into Work Choices without Australian Workplace Agreements (AWAs). The election safely out of the way, it further evolved into a blueprint for making Fair Work Australia the judge of nearly every disagreement between unions and employers.

Sooner or later, the unions that pay Labor's bills and the activists that populate Labor's branches will demand their reward. Disappointed expectations are the big problem that the Rudd Government will have to face. The risk is that people entering the labour market and small business people are likely to feel cheated as the economy worsens. As well, the so-called chattering classes who were so pleased to see the end of John Howard could eventually conclude that Rudd is different, perhaps, but no better. For the moment, being in government is enough to keep the party onside while the pragmatists and managerialists call for reports and try to digest them. Eventually, though, there will be a reckoning between the true believers in unions and big government and the modernisers who want to create a normal centre-left party not institutionally tied to unions or formally committed to nationalisation.

At this stage in the new government's life, it's much easier to see it winning elections than actually making a lasting mark. In style, it's a carbon copy of the NSW Labor government, which has no substantial record despite fourteen years of announcements and photo opportunities. Although it normally takes time for voters to realise that they're being conned, electoral retribution could be swift if people conclude that the new government's policies are making a bad situation worse. That's when the impression Rudd gives of being pleased with himself could quickly turn, in the public's mind, from an understandable pride in being Prime Minister of Australia to insufferable smugness. That's when Rudd's infatuation with appearing on the world stage could seem less like a reflection of the times and more like prime ministerial celebrity tourism and neglect of his real responsibilities.

For the Liberal Party, there's at least as much to be learned from the Howard Government's sustained success as there is from its ultimate defeat. Every government is eventually defeated, but few, if any, governments last as long or achieve as much as Howard's did. Whenever the electoral cycle turns, as inevitably it will, the opposition needs to be a credible alternative. Although the coalition did not have extensive, exhaustively detailed policies going into the 1996 election, there was no doubt about its policy direction. Between 1983 and 1996, due to Howard in large measure, the Liberal Party had become the party of reform. Howard certainly did not 'hit the ground reviewing'.

From the period of the Fraser Government, when he first advocated a GST, until he left office, Howard was the Liberals' deepest and most courageous thinker on Australia's problems and their potential solutions. The Howard Government's policies were not handed to it by the public service or by 'summiteers' shortly after swearing-in. In 1996, Howard made the transition from effective opposition leader to successful prime minister because he had developed a policy framework that touched deep chords in the Australian people as well as a forceful critique of the Keating Government. Financial deregulation, tariff cuts and privatisation, even where implemented by Labor, were Howard ideas first.

One academic commentator described Howard's 1988 Future Directions policy as a 'coherent synthesis of social and economic policies in line with national imperatives'.[7] According to Howard at the time, policy should meet three criteria: does it strengthen the family, give individuals more incentive and hope, and give a preference to private over government enterprise? This combination of smaller government and deregulation with traditional virtues such as thrift, initiative and self-sufficiency reflected Howard's view that social stability was possible, even during radical economic restructuring.[8]

Although the subsequent Fightback! policy released late in 1991 stressed economic reform more, and traditional values less, and was attacked for being too risky rather than too conservative, it was an even more thorough-going policy response to the problems of the time. It was preceded by a formal community-consultation exercise, involving submissions and public meetings, in which individuals and organisations were invited to put forward their views on building a better Australia.

At the 1993 Fightback! election, the Liberals gave the impression that they had studied Australia's problems and now had the answers, whether Australians liked them or not. By 1996, under Howard, the party's policy orientation had been tempered by pragmatism and was certainly expressed in more genial terms. In classic conservative fashion, the Howard Government undersold its changes, presenting huge policy shifts as matter-of-fact responses to different circumstances. Howard's critics could never quite decide whether he was an ogre for changing everything or a wimp for changing nothing. Even now, Labor can't quite decide whether Howard was an economic fraud who should have built even higher surpluses or a flinty 'neo-liberal' who thought there was no such thing as society.

As opposition leader, John Howard's great political achievement was to combine an effective critique of the ALP with a clear program for government. In opposition, he never criticised the then government for spending too little or privatising too much. In government, he never sounded like a former opposition leader without a new script. The Howard Government turned out to be Australia's best postwar exponent of successfully managing the politics of change.

Why was Howard (with his team) more successful than earlier leaders with, in at least some cases, more obvious charisma and fewer long-term critics? First, he had strong values and instincts against which to judge political circumstances; second, he entered government with well-developed policy ideas to address serious national problems; and, finally, he had been both toughened and mellowed by adversity. By the time of his second stint as opposition leader, he had both a first-rate political mind and a first-rate political temperament.

Political leadership is not like running a company or being captain of a ship. Prime ministers can direct public servants, but, for all their prominence and influence, they can rarely give orders to their colleagues. Howard understood that respect had to be earned, affection had to be won, and authority had to be used sparingly if it was to be effective. For an impossibly busy man, he was very good at staying in touch with colleagues when it mattered. For almost twelve years he sufficiently placated the ambitious and the discontented to keep the government together. He massaged big egos so they felt that they were a valued part of a team that others actually led. He accommodated the idealism of people with quite diverse outlooks on life. This is an exhausting balancing act that would test the patience of Job, the wisdom of Solomon, and the capacity of a Mother Teresa to see good in everyone. It also requires the physical stamina of a practised long-distance runner. Howard's ability to be a successful prime minister for almost twelve years is the supreme personal achievement of modern Australian politics.

His senior colleagues' magnanimity helped too. Despite the obvious temptation, Peter Costello refrained from challenging Howard, not from any lack of 'ticker' but from a sense of obligation to the party and the government. No one who watched Costello in the parliament, where he was the most effective hunter-killer of his generation, could doubt his determination or courage. In the end, he wouldn't wreck the government in order to lead it.

It was disappointing but understandable that Costello declined to become leader after the former government's defeat. Costello could have remained on the backbench while he rediscovered his enthusiasm for politics and waited for an opportune time finally to lead the party. Instead, he eventually concluded that his continued presence would destabilise any other leader. It can't have been easy for him again to put his party first. By announcing that he would not re-contest his seat, Costello sacrificed his final chance to become party leader to improve Malcolm Turnbull's chance of winning the next election. Costello wouldn't challenge Turnbull for the leadership or, alternatively, wait until Turnbull's time had passed. It was a fair call but a disappointment to everyone who thought that he still had more to offer public life.

Costello can look back on a career of almost unique achievement. While no important decision can be taken without the support of the head of government, prime ministers don't run departments (other than their own), lack the time to supervise policy detail and certainly can't turn dud ministers into effective managers. Costello can take at least as much credit as his former leader for Australia's best economic years. Prime ministers are the champions of the national interest. Treasurers are the custodians of prudent financial management. It's a thankless task—picking holes in every other cabinet minister's submission and opposing nearly all spending proposals—but it has to be done well if a government is to succeed. The overall quality of the Howard Government's decision-making depended as much on Costello's forensic skills as on Howard's intuition.

It's the nature of modern politics that the work of the team is often obscured by the pivotal role of the captain. Still, it's very hard to be a successful prime minister without effective senior ministers. Howard's senior colleagues were not only highly competent but, from Costello down, were not habitually 'difficult' and showed a rare-in-politics readiness to put the government's interests before their own. Peter Reith and Nick Minchin were effective political warriors and invariably imperturbable under attack. For all Reith's joking about being 'born to plot', he was the least ego-driven and self-absorbed senior politician imaginable. Alexander Downer's quirky sense of humour and irrepressibility made him an important personal support for the prime minister, especially when Howard was under pressure. His and Howard's values and political instincts were almost identical, which helped to make him a very effective foreign minister. National Party leaders Tim Fischer, John Anderson and Mark Vaile knew that a strong conservative coalition would be better for country people in the long run than a party of rural resentment stressing its separate identity.

Although Philip Ruddock had never been considered a close Howard ally, as immigration minister and then attorney-general he turned out to be one of the most effective members of the government. His prodigious administrative efficiency kept a series of complex and sensitive portfolios very well managed. Although his public presentations were steady and thorough, to the point of being long-winded, in cabinet he was concise and incisive and sometimes ended up clarifying issues that others had left confused. It was a terrible calumny to say that he had lost his conscience, let alone his liberal principles, in the administration of the government's border-protection and national-security policies. It's easy for those who don't have to take responsibility for decisions to assume the best of people. Ruddock had to balance the rights of detainees against the rights of the Australian public. Unavoidably, he had to entrust the implementation of policy to a small army of officials and contractors, some of whom, inevitably, made mistakes under pressure. The ethical response to moral blackmail, such as the lip-sewing protests, was not to give in but to ensure that the processing system was working as quickly and as fairly as possible. It's often forgotten that long-term detention was invariably the result of appeals by people who wouldn't take 'no' for an answer.

One of the strengths of the Howard Government was that its senior members left their ideological typecasting at the cabinet cloakroom. Amanda Vanstone could be relied upon to provide a 'women's' perspective if necessary but otherwise brought a practical common sense to the consideration of political problems. For all his reputation as a flinty right-winger, Minchin was every inch the careful electoral politician on, for instance, industry protection or nuclear issues. After one cabinet discussion, the prime minister even remarked of me that I was really an 'arch-pragmatist'.

Howard was a highly effective manager of cabinet. Meetings always started on time and were rarely interrupted by more pressing prime ministerial business or rescheduled because discussions couldn't be concluded. Mostly, Howard would ask the relevant minister to give a précis of the decision sought, then invite comment from around the table. It was unusual for the prime minister to cut off loquacious colleagues, although, because others had a tendency to cut in on verbose contributions, most ministers tended to speak only when they had something worth saying. When cabinet was clearly divided, Howard would usually take a vote. Very occasionally, he would exercise his casting vote against the majority. On particularly difficult or important matters, the prime minister would sometimes state a position from the outset. Colleagues were then welcome to disagree and quite often did, but the position that Howard had arrived at invariably turned out to have broad support. Naturally, members of the Howard cabinet were aware that the prime minister could never be 'rolled' without creating a crisis. For his part, the prime minister appreciated that the relevant minister needed to be convincing in presenting the government's case. Discussion was often robust, sometimes impassioned, but I doubt that ministers ever felt that they hadn't been treated with respect even when their recommendations were rejected.

Because the role of other ministers is to pick holes in your argument, wherever possible I tried to avoid taking decisions to cabinet. On every occasion that I did, though, the ultimate decision was the better for my colleagues' attention. The prime minister usually made a point of congratulating ministers who strongly presented in public decisions they had argued against in private.

Effective political leadership means managing decisions through myriad meetings. As well as cabinet, there were, for instance, weekly party room and daily leadership group meetings while parliament was sitting, plus innumerable meetings with officials and people pleading a cause. Howard had the gift of letting people know what he thought while always seeming to take others' views seriously. He accepted that even prime ministers don't always get their way. The smaller the meeting, the more collegial he usually was. I can only remember one meeting where prime ministerial nerves seemed seriously frayed. It was in the week after APEC to hammer out a form of words about the leadership succession. It could easily have degenerated into an occasion to let off steam. Instead, the customary courtesy of the government's senior members quickly re-asserted itself and a collective position was agreed that best secured the national interest as we then saw it. Even staring defeat in the face, the government never lost its discipline and professionalism.

Arthur Sinodinos and Tony Nutt at the top of the prime minister's office were a formidable duo. Because he knew Howard's mind so well, Sinodinos could stand in for him in many unofficial contexts and, for much of the government's term, was a kind of associate prime minister. He also had the priceless asset of being totally unflappable under pressure.

In a successful political enterprise, people don't have to like each other, but they have to be able to work together and, in particular, avoid bitching about their colleagues behind their backs. The surest sign of a government in disarray is people 'backgrounding' against their leader or ministers leaking against each other. Effective government often means unofficial releases of information, but, in the seven years I was there, I can only recall two actual leaks from cabinet.

Although the public focus is almost entirely on the leader, countless other relationships need to be in working order if the government is not to be distracted. In 1998, after two years as a parliamentary secretary, in those days a kind of ministerial understudy role, I was eager to have some actual decision-making authority. On my first day as his junior minister, it was Peter Reith, not me, who chaired an officials' meeting addressing a funding crisis in the Job Network, even though it was my immediate responsibility. The next morning I fronted my ministerial boss to say that I had no intention of remaining a glorified errand boy. Reith, I suspect, had rather relished the prospect of solving the Job Network's then financial problems but readily agreed that he would leave it to me. He expected to be kept informed of major developments and was happy to offer counsel if sought but would only intervene if I was making a hash of things. Reith, in fact, acted as a political 'elder brother' to many of his colleagues and was a big loss to the government after the 2001 election.

The key reasons for the former government's sustained success were: a leader who stood for something; a team that respected each other; and specific policies that reflected widely held values and addressed the big problems Australia faced. Timing was important, too. In his first stint as opposition leader, Howard had famously remarked that 'the times would suit him'. Howard had mellowed but not fundamentally changed when he became leader for the second time. By then, though, the times had changed in ways that better suited his remarkably constant political character. People were sick of the grandstanding and arrogance of the Keating Government. They wanted a leader who didn't find ordinary Australians an embarrassment and they elected someone who seemed to have the qualities of the Australian 'every man', only to an extraordinary extent.

One night in October 1997, Howard addressed a Liberal Party dinner at the Harbord Diggers Club in my electorate. The government was struggling in the polls. Many even suspected that it would be a 'one-term wonder'. The local MP, as it happened, was still annoyed about being ignored in a reshuffle the previous week. The venue was something of a Labor stronghold in a largely Liberal area. As Howard was leaving the club, he was mobbed—not politely acknowledged, not waved at, not applauded, not cheered, but mobbed. Dozens of people pressed around wanting to touch him. It was a slowly moving scrum of pokie players, 10 p.m. drinkers and cheap-night-out people who thought that the prime minister was one of them. No doubt some of it was the excitement that attaches to a celebrity in a crowd. Most of it, though, was the chord that this not-obviously-charismatic man had struck in so many of the Australian people.

Paul Keating once said that 'if you change the prime minister, you change the country'. It's equally true that if you change the leader, you change the party. John Howard led the Liberal Party for seventeen years, almost as long as Menzies and twice as long as Malcolm Fraser. The Liberal Party is now frequently referred to as a small 'c' 'conservative party' by many of its senior members. In Menzies' day, only the party's critics would have described it that way. Although the Liberal Party has always been the Australian custodian of both the liberal and the conservative tradition, it took Howard to publicly and frequently acknowledge it.

In his 'Howard's Brutopia' essay, Rudd claimed that there was a fundamental contradiction between the former prime minister's respect for traditional social values and his government's alleged commitment to dog-eat-dog capitalism. Rudd's analysis of the former prime minister's political doctrine was a caricature at best. In any event, at least in the English-speaking political tradition, the tensions between liberalism and conservatism, between traditional values and a market economy, are more apparent than real, as I will attempt to demonstrate in the next chapter.

3 What's Right?

In 1996, Pauline Hanson's maiden speech echoed round the country. 'At last', said millions of people listening to Hanson's complaints about Aborigines, migrants and foreign corporations, 'someone is brave enough to say what I think'. Largely written by right-wing maverick John Pasquarelli, it was a conservative outsider's cry of rage and fear. As talk-back radio support took off for the former fish-and-chip shop owner and disendorsed Liberal candidate and as she began to speak at well-attended public meetings, millions of other Australians came to the opposite conclusion: that we really might be a racist country, frightened of change and stuck in the past.

For the newly elected prime minister, this was a fraught development. The post–Port Arthur massacre gun laws had alienated many country people. Some of those who'd most loathed Paul Keating thought that nothing much was changing and feared that they'd elected another do-little conservative like Malcolm Fraser. Hanson attacked Howard for not standing up, as she put it, for the 'real Australia'. On the other hand, the former Keating cheer squad attacked him for allegedly being a closet Hansonite himself. A few members of his own party wanted him to sound more like Hanson to undermine her appeal to conservative voters. Others wanted him to attack Hanson so that the whole country would understand that her views were outside the boundaries of acceptable public discourse. For his part, Howard consistently disagreed with her critique of modern Australia but almost never directly or personally criticised her. He wanted people to understand that her views were often wrong and nearly always over the top but that he understood the concerns of the people who were listening to her.

In June 1998 the real impact of the Hanson movement became clear. In the Queensland election, eleven One Nation MPs won seats that would otherwise have returned coalition candidates and, consequently, a state Labor government was elected. The impact of the Hanson party had been to take votes away from the only conservatives who were ever likely to be in power. From that point, it should have been obvious that voting for Hanson would not produce a more hardline conservative movement but a more divided one. In other words, Hanson had the clear potential to turn Labor into the automatic party of government.

On the Friday after the Queensland election, I published an op-ed article pointing out the threat that Hansonism posed to intelligent conservatism and urging the Liberal Party to put One Nation candidates last on its how-to-votes. It was designed to prevent my anxious colleagues from flirting with a movement that could ultimately destroy them. Over the next parliamentary sitting fortnight, the last before the 1998 federal election, I made a series of parliamentary speeches pointing out that One Nation was a company owned by three directors rather than a political party democratically controlled by its members. These speeches were meant to alert voters to the real nature of the Hanson movement. In the last of these speeches, I said that, as a company with three shareholders rather than as a party with more than 500 members, One Nation might not have been legally entitled to the public funding it had received for the result in the Queensland election.

For me, the problem with Hanson was not just that she was making non-Anglo Australians feel like strangers in their own country. I also felt some personal responsibility for the rise of this mutant form of conservatism. After the 1996 election, as a way of making peace within a divided local Liberal Party, I'd employed a former candidate for the state seat of Manly, David Oldfield, as my private secretary. Oldfield was capable and intensely ambitious but, at least in those days, had a brutal way of expressing views that were teetering over the edge of respectability. I'd thought that working for me might turn him into more of a team player. Instead, he began secretly moonlighting for Hanson. He supplanted Pasquarelli to become, as I said at the time, more than a mentor: Hanson's 'Rasputin' or 'human autocue'. Having unwittingly helped to give birth to One Nation, I felt a personal duty to stop people being taken in by it.

Subsequently, I helped a disgruntled former One Nation candidate to take legal action to recover the $500,000 in public funding improperly given to the private company masquerading as a political party. Long after sacking the pro-bono lawyers I had provided for him, representing himself in court, Terry Sharples won the case. Much later, the Queensland DPP brought criminal charges against Hanson for, he alleged, fraudulently claiming this money. She was convicted and briefly went to jail before being freed on appeal. To the Beattie Labor government keen to escape blame, to Hanson admirers and even to the politically correct inquisitors who'd once demanded her excommunication, she now became another victim of the Howard Government. She certainly didn't deserve to be jailed for what was a political rather than a criminal scam. By that time, she was no longer taken seriously as a politician but certainly had the consolation of some wider public sympathy.

For me, the campaign against Hanson had turned out to be a messy business. To some, I'd more or less personally jailed her. For years I was hounded by Sharples, who claimed I'd breached a commitment to him. When I didn't immediately volunteer to an interviewer all the details of who had been helping to support the original Sharples case, this was taken to be 'misleading the ABC'. Making light of this got me into even more trouble. Still, One Nation's 22 per cent vote in the 1998 Queensland election had dropped to just 8 per cent in the federal election three months later. What turned out to be Australia's most effective conservative government survived thanks, in part, to my warnings about the impact of voting for One Nation.

The sudden (if temporary) rise of One Nation showed the potential power of populism even in a mature and stable democracy like Australia. There are essentially two types of conservative: those who fear change and instinctively resist it, and those who respect the society that's made them and want the future to reflect the best aspects of the past. The Hanson movement and the different reactions to it helped to illuminate the differences between fearful and hopeful conservatism and the swirling mix of populism and high principle that could co-exist even within voters, let alone inside political parties. Most One Nation voters eventually returned to the Liberal and National Parties, partly because they saw through Hanson and partly because the economy continued to improve but also, I suspect, because the Howard Government became better at demonstrating its conservative as well as its liberal credentials.

Trying to keep 'doctors' wives', Howard battlers and Hanson 'rednecks' more or less inside the same 'broad church' (as Howard called it) or 'big tent' (which was John Brogden's phrase) is no easy task when in government, and is even harder when in opposition, but is essential if the coalition is to win elections. Oppositions can change their mind, but they can't change the country. Governments have to focus on building a better Australia; oppositions tend to focus on themselves. Governments have decisions to make; oppositions have opinions to put forward. Opinions tend to be especially precious to those who have little else to flaunt. It's why oppositions often have what seem like theological disputes about comparatively minor points. The more passionately these disputes are pursued, the more divided and directionless an opposition party often seems.

In government, politicians are dealing with specific problems or policy challenges. Options are debated, answers formulated and decisions implemented (as best they can be). In government, MPs who might have preferred a different approach to a particular problem will soon have another issue to come to grips with. In opposition, by contrast, little is ever finally decided because all opposition MPs really have is their votes, which are often inconsequential and can always change. Governments decide what to do. Oppositions decide what to say. Opinions can be revised in a way that deeds can't. In opposition, philosophical arguments assume much more significance because an opposition's job is to clarify its own thinking rather than actually to govern the country.

One of the big temptations for a new opposition is to try to save the country from the wrong side of the parliament. If the opposition is convinced that the government's legislation is wrong and almost the entire country is clamouring for a bill's defeat, it would make sense to vote against it in the Senate. What more often happens, though, is that the opposition votes against bills reflecting the policies on which the government has fought an election. Under these circumstances, voters usually wonder whether the opposition has learned the lessons of defeat; and governments always demand to know, chapter and verse, the opposition's alternative. If the opposition successfully blocks legislation, the government has a double benefit: it can continue to support poor policies without having to face up to their disastrous consequences. If, on the other hand, the government's legislation still passes, the opposition tends to look obstructionist and clueless.

Oppositions tend to be damned if they do and damned if they don't, especially new ones. What is the point of opposing legislation when it is likely to pass anyway; or, if not, the opposition will be saving voters from the consequences of their own choice? An opposition that's threatening to block legislation is relevant, but it usually then becomes the issue without—once the government has sought a deal with minor parties and independents—actually bringing about the desired result. An opposition that negotiates with the government, on the other hand, in order to improve a flawed bill usually ends up sharing responsibility for legislation it basically doesn't like. There's much to be said for adopting the view that the government is generally entitled to get its legislation through, because that's what the people voted for. It frees the opposition from needing a position on everything that's contentious. It minimises the potential for internal division, maximises the pressure on the government and gives the opposition the most breathing space in which to develop new policies of its own. Stating a general disposition can license some departures from it; trying to remain totally flexible just makes the opposition look unprincipled and opportunist.

Relatively new oppositions have nearly always been a disappointment to their supporters. John Stone, for instance, in a recent speech to the HR Nicholls Society, has criticised the Liberal Party for allegedly not standing for anything except the politically correct and unrepresentative values of 'Wentworth man'. At least in the early days of opposition, it was ever thus. In 1985, for instance, BA Santamaria complained that 'nobody can any longer define what the Liberal Party stands for or even if it stands for anything'.[1] Santamaria had been close enough to Malcolm Fraser to have welcomed the then Liberal prime minister to the Sydney and Melbourne events marking the fortieth anniversary of the National Civic Council. The extent of his disillusionment, just two years after the Fraser Government's defeat, is a sign of the uncertainty and revisionism that seems to grip all political parties in the aftermath of an election loss, and their supporters even more. It's equally characteristic of political parties that the prospect of victory tends to dispel this kind of existential doubt. The only really happy opposition is one that's convinced it's on the verge of winning government.

In the wake of the party's loss to Gough Whitlam, even its founder, Sir Robert Menzies, had lamented that the 'party of everybody' had become the 'party of nothing'.[2] Although Santamaria had never been an uncritical admirer of the Liberal Party (to put it mildly), he was in little doubt about what it stood for during the Menzies, Fraser and Howard prime ministerships. What the Liberal Party needed to do, he'd said back in 1985, was to rededicate itself to 'patriotism ... the family ... the small unit in agriculture, industry and commerce ... political obligation ... intellectual rigour'.[3] The fact that, in 1998, Prime Minister Howard was almost the dying political warrior's last visitor suggests that, for the third time, there had been a rapprochement of sorts between the Liberal Party and the ultimate true believer of Australian politics.

It should not be especially surprising that Santamaria discerned a political spine in the Menzies, Fraser and Howard Governments in their prime, but not in the intervening Liberal oppositions. Whatever a political party's principles might be, they're validated, in a sense, by an election victory. By contrast, a defeated party must go through a period of introspection, if only to keep faith with the electorate that has rejected it. This is what Menzies was driving at when he wrote that defeat 'disunites the defeated'.[4] Unless they're to thumb their noses at the electorate, newly defeated parties have to reconsider their policies and, in the process, to refine their principles.

Defeated political parties have no alternative but to engage in a period of soul-searching, because successful oppositions have to redefine themselves in the period before winning office. Provided it never comes to the point of protagonists refusing to speak to each other, argument over the party's direction is less a regrettable sign of confusion than a healthy response to reality. Of course, a new consensus must eventually emerge, but there should be a debate first. The party's values and direction can't be taken for granted, assumed to be self-evident or imposed from on high. Inevitably, that debate will sometimes be politically awkward, but suppressing it or trying to rush it normally stores up worse problems for the future. Internal debate can actually be a sign that the process of renewal has begun. People's readiness to discuss what a party stands for often means that they are once more starting to take its prospects seriously.

Romanticising the achievements of the previous government and demanding that the electorate repent of its mistake is a recipe for a very long stint in opposition. Another common error is to re-litigate the internal disputes of an earlier time or even to view the defeated government as an aberration, out of step with the party's true spirit and greatest leaders. All successful leaders have something to teach succeeding generations. All of them, though, are successful in their own time and under their own circumstances. The next successful Liberal prime minister will no more be a clone of John Howard than Howard was himself a clone of Bob Menzies or Malcolm Fraser.

Since the 2007 election, commentators such as Robert Manne and even frontbenchers such as George Brandis have claimed that Howard had moved the Liberal Party too far to the 'right'. To succeed, they say, the party should return to the philosophically small 'l' liberal tradition of former Prime Ministers Menzies or Alfred Deakin. This rather overlooks the fact that Deakin's main prime ministerial legacies were problematical ones: industrial arbitration and the White Australia policy. For his part, Menzies sought to ban the Communist Party and famously gushed over the young Queen Elizabeth, 'I did but see her passing by and yet I love her till I die'. It ought to be clear that Howard's great political forebears can't easily be categorised. In any event, it's idle to claim the glorious dead, who never had to deal with contemporary circumstances and who can now be 'verballed' with impunity, as authority for one's own position.

In a perceptive essay, Sam Roggeveen says that the 'real difference between conservatives and liberals is that conservatives have not been infected with the spirit of improvement'. Conservatives, he says, feel no particular need to justify the status quo. The adage 'if it's not necessary to change, it's necessary not to change' perhaps best captures this spirit. By contrast, says Roggeveen, liberals regard anything that can't be justified as essentially provisional until something more convincing can be devised.[5] This is a helpful distinction at least on some issues, such as the monarchy, which is probably the best litmus test for whether people stand within the Liberal Party's conservative or liberal traditions. To liberals, the monarchy tends to be dispensable because it can be made to appear a historical accident or even offensive to anti-discrimination principles. To conservatives, on the other hand, apart from its being a subtle and stable system, 'the heart has reasons that reason cannot know'.

It's by no means an infallible test, though. Peter Costello, a monarchist who became a reluctant republican, is conservative on most social issues. George Brandis, by contrast, who is generally socially liberal, was reportedly the only participant in the 2020 Summit to support the Crown. In my judgment, a big majority of Liberal MPs are instinctive traditionalists on social issues but broadly pro-market on economic issues. A small but vocal group of MPs tend to be libertarian on social issues and would be inclined to support, for instance, on harm-minimisation grounds, initiatives such as drug-injecting rooms. A somewhat larger group could perhaps be described as economic traditionalists reluctant, for instance, to support change that might harm socially important industries.

Even so, internal tension often owes more to the company people keep than to the philosophies they hold. The history of the SA Liberal Party, for instance, keeps Nick Minchin and Christopher Pyne in opposite camps, even though on 'life' issues they invariably vote the same way. Animosities within the NSW Liberal Party meant that John Howard and influential former frontbencher Bronwyn Bishop were never particularly close, even though their philosophical instincts were almost indistinguishable. In any event, the differences between most people who regard themselves as liberal and most who regard themselves as conservative inside the Liberal Party, however sharp, are seldom incapable of resolution. Indeed, a litmus test for effective Liberal leadership is finding meaningful common ground between the party's more liberal and more conservative tendencies.

At least since Edmund Burke defined a political party as a 'body of men ... promoting by their joint endeavours the national interest upon some particular principle in which they are all agreed', politicians in the same party have often argued over what their core principles really are. Articulating and defining the precise principles and philosophies that their leading members have in common is no easy task for a broad-based political party. All too often, the result of such an exercise, if not a furious row, turns out to be a motherhood statement. In political shorthand, 'socialist' parties might stand for government control of the economy, 'liberal' parties for individual freedom and 'conservative' parties for traditional institutions. Still, their members usually wrestle, at times convulsively, with precisely what these concepts might really mean and how far they should be taken.

Political liberalism is no more easily reduced to a neat political prescription than any other major political philosophy. For one thing, John Stuart Mill, the great philosopher of liberalism, espoused quite different political positions at different times in his life. The Mill of *On Liberty* stressed the greatest possible freedom of the individual consistent with the like liberty of others. At other times and in other works, he stressed the importance of government intervention to create equality of opportunity and even equality of outcome. Australian liberalism's multi-faceted personality is reflected in the different federation-era political programs supported, on the one hand, by Alfred Deakin and, on the other, by his philosophically important but now little remembered contemporary Bruce Smith.

In his *Short History of Australian Liberalism*, the Wollongong University historian Greg Melleuish cites Deakin's approving description of an Australian liberal as 'one who favours state interference with liberty and industry at the pleasure and in the interest of the majority'.[6] Melleuish contrasts this with Smith's view of liberalism: that public revenue should only be spent, private property only interfered with and personal liberty only restricted to secure the equal freedom of all citizens.[7] Melleuish further cites early-twentieth-century Prime Minister Sir George Reid's approving description of an Australian conservative as one who supports 'allowing the genius for competition, for excelling, for acquiring to reach its utmost altitude consistent with the due rights of others'.[8]

Australia's first Liberal Party, formed in 1909 to unify the non-Labor political forces, included all three of these individuals and had to incorporate their different philosophical approaches. There was, though, much overlap between Reid's conservatism, Smith's liberalism and Deakin's hostility to a party controlled by trade unions. In a statement that most Australian liberals as well as most Australian conservatives could have broadly supported, Bernard Wise—perhaps Australia's first significant conservative thinker—declared that there were three tests to be applied when considering an action of the state: it ought not 'weaken the motives for morality', it 'should not do that which might be done as well by private persons' and it 'should never act in such a way as to weaken individual self-reliance'.[9]

Outsiders typically make two mistakes about the Liberal Party. First, they read too much into its name and assume that it has a doctrinaire commitment to a particular concept of freedom. Second, once they discover that the party is instinctively conservative as well as liberal, they discount its chances of electoral success on the grounds that Australians lack a well-developed appreciation of their past. On my first visit to the United States after becoming an MP, I was described as a 'strong Liberal' and 'very anti-republican', so most of my hosts thought I was a virtual communist! In a 2006 speech, the party's federal director told an American audience that he was 'often asked' about the party's name. The Australian Liberal Party has certainly inherited many of the values of Britain's eighteenth-century Whigs but has little in common with the contemporary UK Liberal Party. Still, the fact that others maybe insufficiently aware of the strength of the conservative tradition inside the party is no reason for Australian Liberals to minimise it.

As John Howard has frequently observed, in this country the Liberal Party is the political custodian of both the liberal and the conservative traditions. As a consequence, to maintain its coherence on policy, the Liberal Party has had not only to manage the tensions inside these two different orientations but also to reconcile each to the other. Given this daunting challenge, it's not surprising that critics can often find evidence to justify accusations that the party stands for nothing, stands for inconsistent things, or has suppressed elements of its own tradition. Even so, contention over what it 'really stands for' has no more been an electoral obstacle for the Liberal Party than for the Labor Party, which has had its own varied philosophical orientations to manage.

Political parties' policy orientation often only becomes apparent in government. It was clear that the Menzies Opposition opposed rationing, bank nationalisation and communist influence in the union movement, but few would have predicted, in 1949, that the Menzies Government's principal legacies would turn out to be the expansion of universities and the extension of the Commonwealth government's authority within the federation. It was clear that the Fraser Opposition opposed profligate spending and maladministration, but few would have predicted, in 1975, that its legacy would be the consolidation of Whitlam Government policies such as multiculturalism. In 1983, almost no one would have imagined that the Hawke Government's legacy would be financial deregulation and tariff cuts.

By contrast, in 1996, many expected that the Howard Government would introduce a GST, privatisation and far-reaching industrial change because these figured in Labor's pre-election scare campaign. The key difference between the Liberal Party's period in opposition between 1983 and 1996 and its earlier stints in opposition, at least in the second half of this period, was the emphasis given to policy development and the extensive reflection on values and objectives that this necessitated. The so-called 'wet' versus 'dry' struggles caused much political embarrassment at the time, but they helped to define John Howard's political personality and ultimately left the party with an agreed agenda that largely guided the Howard Government.

An opposition party's main day-to-day task is always to mount an effective critique of the government. Sometimes, though, poor governments are re-elected because of doubts about the opposition. Constructing a clear alternative, therefore, is almost as important for an opposition as attacking the government, especially as an election draws closer. The next Liberal government won't need to assume office with specific policies on all topics down to the last detail. Too much detail can easily give the government material for a scare campaign. Still, if it is to be an effective opposition, it will need some policies that have been clearly thought through and tested in public debate, so that voters have a definite impression of how it should be different from and better than Labor.

The task is to prioritise the country's most pressing problems and to devise practical remedies that reflect the party's enduring values and principles. The Liberal Party has a natural preference for freedom. Still, the extent to which the contemporary party is relatively 'liberal' or 'conservative' will best be determined by considering the policies that it develops rather than by arguing over what it ought to be in the abstract. As Menzies pointed out in his memoirs, 'there was to be nothing doctrinaire about our policies. If I were to become the leader of a great non-Socialist party, I must look at everything in a practical way'.[10] This, I'm sure, is what the then Liberal leader John Hewson was driving at when he declared, in his 1990 Menzies Lecture, that 'liberalism ... the search for freedom, means very little unless it is firmly placed in the context of real problems faced by real people'.

Although all its most important leaders have discussed the party's principles, none of them have been prescriptive about their pecking order. Certainly, the Liberal Party would not have been so politically successful if it had simply been 'liberal'. A century ago, Smith's 'pure' liberalism (as he saw it) meant opposing government involvement in poverty relief, education and most public works. For all freedom's resonance, an ideological commitment to minimal government, come what may, would be of limited electoral appeal.

In an oft-quoted passage from his memoirs, Menzies recalls the party's formation: 'We took the name "Liberal" because we were determined to be a progressive party, willing to make experiments, in no sense reactionary, but believing in the individual, his rights and his enterprise'.[11] This passage is often cited as a conclusive argument against those Liberals whose orientation is more conservative. It's worth noting, though, that Menzies, in his very next sentence, goes on to differentiate his sense of what 'liberal' means from its meaning in America, where, he says, 'the word "liberal" is used in contradistinction to "conservative"'.

Even though Menzies himself never used the term 'conservative' to describe the party he formed, he clearly did not intend it to be anti-conservative in the sense that an American 'liberal' is typically anti-conservative. As well, there is little doubt about the presence of a strong conservative streak in Menzies' own political character. He stressed the 'creative genius of the individual' but also the need for the individual to be 'assisted and sometimes controlled by the government in the general social interest'. It was the responsible, not the irresponsible individual who was the 'real basis of a truly free society'.[12] Likewise, he believed in a 'free and encouraged private enterprise' but not 'irresponsible enterprise'. In his famous *Forgotten People* radio broadcasts, Menzies spoke of 'homes spiritual' and 'homes material'. In his 1949 election launch, he said that the 'real freedoms are to worship, to think, to speak, to choose, to be ambitious, to be independent, to be industrious, to acquire skill, to seek reward ... for these are of the essence, of the nature of man ... Are we for the socialist state ... or are we for the ancient British faith that governments are the servants of the people, a faith that has given fire and quality and direction to the whole of our history for 600 years'. On such evidence, the former journalist, Hewson biographer, and Liberal staffer Norman Abjorensen characterises Menzies as a 'consensual conservative', at least as a means of distinguishing him from John Howard.[13]

In a fine speech delivered to the SA Liberal Party in 1980, Malcolm Fraser explored the necessary relationship that liberalism had with conservatism as well as the tensions between them. 'Once liberal institutions are installed in a society, a government which wishes to preserve them must be in some sense conservative', he said. Liberalism, he said, 'always emphasises the freedom of the individual and the absence of restraint ... Conservatism, on the other hand, stresses the need for a framework of stability, continuity and order not only as something desirable in itself but as a necessary condition for a free society'. Fraser concluded that 'the art of handling this tension, of finding that creative balance between the forces of freedom and the forces of continuity which alone allows a society to advance, is the true art of government in a country like ours'.[14]

Although Australians had long spoken of the 'conservative side of politics', Fraser seems to have been the first Liberal prime minister to allow his government to be described as a 'conservative' one. The governor-general's 1980 address to the opening of parliament described a government that was 'liberal in its principles' but 'conservative in its distrust of abrupt and sweeping changes'.[15]

In acknowledging the debt that liberalism owes to conservatism, Fraser grasped a truth that has eluded many distinguished thinkers, even the great FA Hayek. In his well-known essay 'Why I Am Not a Conservative', Hayek pays tribute to conservatism as a 'legitimate, probably necessary and certainly widespread attitude of opposition to drastic change' but claims that it 'cannot offer an alternative to the direction in which we are moving'.[16] To Hayek, conservatism was about the speed of change, not its direction. He made the common mistake of assuming that conservatism is more the cast of mind that's resistant to change than a body of ideas or a set of principles. The fact that other doctrines can advance in a conservative way does not mean that there is no specific conservatism with its own basic propositions and doctrine.

Political conservatism is not content-less, even though it's not as readily reducible to a single key policy idea, as liberalism or socialism might be, and can sometimes seem elastic enough to mean whatever the speaker wants it to. In one of his novels, Benjamin Disraeli said that Toryism would 'bring back strength to the Crown, liberty to the subject, and … announce that power has only one duty, to secure the social welfare of the people'.[17] In a recent speech, the British Conservative leader David Cameron said that fairness, equal opportunity, a concern for the environment, and a safer society are at the heart of what he called 'progressive conservatism'.[18] This means, he said, policies that devolve responsibility to individuals and civic institutions, support the family, foster economic growth, and ensure that government lives within its means. In an earlier speech, he had said that 'practical conservatism' meant 'more police, school discipline, cleaner hospitals, controlled immigration and lower taxes'.[19]

In a brilliant paper, 'What Is a Conservative?', the British commentator Paul Johnson said that 'there can be all kinds of Conservatives; always have been, always will be. There is no archetype; no workable definition. In a way, Conservatives find the same problem in defining themselves as the founding fathers of Israel when they tried to define a Jew. In the end, they decided that anyone was a Jew who thought himself, and called himself, a Jew'. On the other hand, in a later article for *The Spectator*, Johnson declared that 'there are six indispensable hallmarks of a conservative. First, firm belief in one, beneficent and omnipotent God. Second, absolute morality as the basis of public law. Third, strict limits on the size of the state. Fourth, respect for a multiplicity of traditional power centres. Fifth, restraint and self-restraint in all things. Sixth, search for the right balance between the individual and the traditional units of society … There is a seventh point.

A conservative is not afraid of force, or of using it thoroughly. But always as a last resort'.[20]

John Ray, an academic writing in the 1970s, seems to have been the first Australian to have described himself as a 'Burkean conservative', after the late-18th-century British statesman rightly regarded as the founder of modern political conservatism. 'I believe that the Vietnam War can be justified', Ray said:

> that conscription can be necessary, that most ecology activists are cranks, that the 20th century is the best century we have ever had and that the 21st will be even better, that economic growth is a good thing, that strikers who defy the courts should be outlawed, that the White Australia policy is defensible, that Ian Smith of Rhodesia is neither a fool nor a rogue, that our ties with the monarchy are precious and should not be reduced (and) that we should have more foreign investment and continued population growth'.[21]

Of course, not all of these positions would have been held by all conservatives even then.

Robert Blake, the principal historian of British conservatism, has said that, from the 1820s to the 1950s, conservative voters would have had much the same outlook:

> There was a similar belief that Britain, especially England, was usually in the right. There was a similar faith in the value of diversity, of independent institutions, of the rights of property; a similar distrust of centralising officialdom, of the efficacy of government (except in the preservation of order and national defence), of Utopian panaceas and of 'doctrinaire' intellectuals; a similar dislike of abstract ideas, high philosophical principles and sweeping generalisations. There was a similar readiness to accept cautious empirical piecemeal reform, if a conservative government said it was needed. There was a similar reluctance to look far ahead

> or worry too much about the future; a similar scepticism about human nature; and similar belief in original sin and in the limitations of political and social amelioration; … a similar scepticism about the notion of 'equality'.[22]

To some extent, Margaret Thatcher broke that mould, but even her radical program aimed to restore to their proper place in the functioning of society earlier values such as 'competition, a stable currency, self-help, free enterprise … law and order'.[23]

A 'statement of conservatism' posted on the Centreright website on 30 December last year includes these key propositions:

- no insignificant person has ever been born
- economic liberalism needs social conservatism and vice versa
- government should be as small as possible but as large as necessary
- politics is less important than ideas, culture and religion
- free enterprise and big business are not the same
- there is such a thing as society, it's just not the state
- decision-making powers should be as close as possible to those affected by those decisions
- private ownership is nearly always preferable to common ownership
- love of country is fundamental to all conservatism
- private choices have public consequences
- policy makers have an interest in private choices at least so long as they have consequences for taxpayers.

It's worth stressing that few, if any, of these conservative propositions would be objectionable to most people who regard themselves as Australian liberals.

Liberals are inclined to stress freedom as an end in itself. Conservatives are inclined to regard freedom as an important element in a decent and humane society. Liberals are inclined to be impatient with rules. Conservatives think that a framework of rules is necessary if freedom is to be realised. Although particular liberals may have very little in common with particular conservatives, there is much overlap between their broad positions. Conservatives are not against all change. As Burke observed: a state without the means of change is without the means of its own conservation. Disraeli said that 'in a progressive country, change is constant and the question is not whether you should resist change which is inevitable but whether that change should be carried out in deference to the manners, the customs, the laws and the traditions of a people [rather than] … in deference to arbitrary and general doctrines'.[24] Conservatives are not against the operation of market economies, either. After discussing with him his concept of political economy, Adam Smith declared that Burke 'was the only man who, without communication, thought on these topics exactly as [he] did'.[25]

In a celebrated passage from his *Reflections on the Revolution in France*, Burke dwelt on some of the qualifications which conservatives place on freedom:

> I should therefore suspend my congratulations on the new liberty of France until I was informed how it had been combined with government, with public force, with the discipline and obedience of armies, with the collection of an effective and well-distributed revenue, with morality and religion, with the solidity of property, with peace and order, with civil and social manners. All these in their way are good things too and, without them, liberty is not a benefit while it lasts and is not likely to continue long.[26]

Although Burke had declared himself a devotee of a 'manly, moral and well-regulated liberty' because, he said, 'the effect of liberty to individuals is that they may do what they please' we ought 'to see what it will please them to do before we risk congratulations which may be soon turned into complaints'.[27] Freedom, he thought, had to be judged in context because it's 'circumstances which render every civil and political scheme beneficial or noxious to mankind'.

Even to Michael Oakeshott, perhaps its greatest academic exponent, conservatism was as much a state of mind as a developed political philosophy. A kind of conservatism, he says, is not just important but actually necessary:

> Whenever stability is more profitable than improvement … certainty … more valuable than speculation … familiarity … more desirable than perfection … agreed error … superior to controversial truth … the disease … more sufferable than the cure … the satisfaction of expectations more important than the justice of the expectations themselves … a rule of some sort better than the risk of having no rule at all, a disposition to be conservative will be more appropriate than any other.[28]

To Oakeshott, though, political conservatism is not entirely lacking in specific content. It's about limited government and ensuring that a version of due process characterises the political system. A political conservative, says Oakeshott, will prefer allowing individuals and entities to go about their business to any scheme of arrangement imposed by government. To a conservative, he says, the task of government is to be an 'umpire' administering the rules of society or a 'chairman' ensuring that the national conversation remains orderly. To a conservative, government is 'not the management of an enterprise but the rule of those engaged in a great diversity of self-chosen enterprises'.[29] Conservatives will have different opinions about much else but, when it comes to government, they will tend to agree with liberals that its main job is to 'hold the ring'.

Oakeshott notes that conservatism seems to be at odds with the modern mindset which, he says, is 'in love with change'. To contemporary men and women, he says:

> the fascination of what is new is felt far more keenly than the comfort of what is familiar … There is a positive prejudice in favour of the yet untried … Pieties are fleeting, loyalties evanescent, and the pace of change warns us against too deep attachments. We are willing to

> try anything once regardless of the consequences ... discarded motor cars and television sets have their counterparts in discarded moral and religious beliefs; the eye is ever on the new model.[30]

Still, he says, because it allows freedom and diversity (albeit within a framework of rules that have evolved over time), political conservatism is particularly apt for the government of an 'adventurous and enterprising' people. 'It is not at all inconsistent', he says, 'to be conservative in respect of government and radical in respect of almost every other activity.'[31]

Although, self-evidently, not everyone is a political conservative, almost everyone has some conservative instincts. The task of conservative political parties is to show voters how these instincts are relevant to contemporary political issues—more relevant, in fact, than the values to which other political parties are appealing. The ability of the UK Conservative Party and of the 'conservative side of Australian politics' to be in power for fully two thirds of the twentieth century suggests that this is by no means mission impossible. The Rudd Government's continuing popularity has prompted some claims that the electorate has moved to the left.[32] In fact, the ANU's political-values surveys, regularly taken after each election, have shown only a slight diminution of support for conservative positions over the life of the Howard Government. Their most striking and consistent finding has actually been the gulf between the left-wing orientation of Labor MPs and the orientation of the electorate. Of course, many commentators would like the electorate to have shifted, but Kevin Rudd's pre-election insistence on being a conservative of sorts suggests that the most hard-headed political operatives don't think that it has.

In a letter to Disraeli, Lord Derby observed that 'the conservatives are weakest among intellectual classes as is natural'.[33] It's not surprising that people who are temperamentally in favour of the new over the old, change over stability and ferment over order should have little deep understanding of conservatism. This helps to explain the academic tendency to treat conservatism as a bacillus in the body politic and the propensity of academics to identify it with being reactionary. Most academics also make too much of the tension between conservatism and liberalism. The 'conservative side of politics' must be at war with itself, they think, because, like Kevin Rudd in 'Howard's Brutopia', they imagine that its economic policy is simply to 'let the market rip'. To Hayek, economic freedom was the product of social order, not the result of an unfettered free market. Hence, Rudd's thesis not only misjudged Howard but completely misunderstood Hayek.

As Roger Scruton has remarked, approximately half the English people persist in voting Conservative at national elections even though almost all English intellectuals regard 'conservative' as a term of abuse. Scruton, probably the English-speaking world's finest contemporary conservative thinker, evokes a conservatism that's founded on an instinctive love of country.

Conservatives are engaged in their country's history, proud of its symbols, concerned for its welfare, attached to its values and vigorous in its defence. The instinct to defer to authority and to respect tradition—the sense that each individual has been shaped by the past and will influence the future, having both ancestors and descendants to keep faith with—is deeply ingrained in human beings, even if it's grossly under-appreciated by intellectuals. A conservative apprehends how so much modern thinking is actually in revolt against human nature. Conservatives are conscious of both loss and hope. Achievement is possible because 'pygmies are standing on the shoulders of giants'.

Far from just slowing and moderating the pace of change, a political conservative can promote change, provided it's to realise a country's best values and aspirations. Hayek concedes that, in America, for instance, liberals and conservatives might both defend individual liberty. A conservative would do so because liberty is the aim and product of long-established American institutions. On the other hand, a liberal would do so, Hayek contends, 'not mainly because they are long established or because they are American but because they correspond to the ideals which he cherishes'.[34] Would, then, an American conservative cherish dictatorship if that had been the American experience; does a Russian conservative yearn for the good old days of communism? Hayek, presumably, thought that they would because, in his view, conservatism meant opposition to change rather than support for a particular political philosophy. At the risk of taking issue with a philosophical giant, I doubt it very much. Some concept of respect for human dignity (coupled, to be sure, with scepticism about novel ways to advance it) is central to political conservatism the world over.

Hayek also concedes that 'the liberal position shares with conservatism a distrust of reason to the extent that the liberal is very much aware that we do not know all the answers'. The difference, says Hayek, is liberals' willingness 'to admit how little we know without claiming the authority of supernatural sources'.[35] Hayek eventually states that 'the more I learn about the evolution of ideas, the more I have become aware that I am simply an unrepentant old Whig'.[36] With Burke, Hayek believed that certain rules are so deeply embedded (at least in Western culture) that they seem to have been imprinted on the human mind.[37] In the end, there seems to be very little practical difference between a Hayekian liberal and a Burkean conservative. A Hayekian liberal, in fact, might simply be a conservative who no longer believes in God.

Burke supported the American Revolution because it was an attempt to regain in the new world the traditional rights and freedoms of Englishmen. He trenchantly opposed the French Revolution, which he saw as a usurpation of established order in the name of abstract principles that was bound to lead to tyranny. For Burke, the evil of the French Revolution lay in its overturning of all precedent. Hayek adopted much the same attitude, arguing that 'people cannot form a society and then give themselves laws, as Rousseau had imagined'.[38]

At various times, Burke was a member of the government of William Pitt the Younger. Although Pitt was formally a Whig, Johnson calls it Britain's 'first Conservative government in the modern sense'.[39] Pitt supported independence for the American colonies, economic and parliamentary reform, Catholic emancipation, and free trade because, he thought, these reflected the best values and true interests of the

British people. Even so, says Johnson, Burke's parliamentary leader was a conservative: 'in the sense that he believed that evolutionary changes, conducted through the framework of an ancient constitution and through representative bodies like the House of Commons, were infinitely preferable to revolutionary changes detonated by violence'. For conservatives, Johnson, says, 'changes should be brought about in an orderly manner under the rule of law'.[40]

Pitt, it seems, was an 'activist' conservative, a type that would subsequently include Disraeli, Ronald Reagan, Margaret Thatcher and John Howard. These were conservatives who strongly promoted change that could be said to preserve or restore traditional values. Then there were 'incremental' conservatives, who wanted to make the prudent, moderate changes that they thought would strengthen society. Sir Robert Peel and perhaps Menzies and Fraser might be thought of in this category. Edward Heath ended up a relatively unsuccessful exemplar of this type, even though he had originally wanted to embark on 'a change so radical, a revolution ... so total that it will go far beyond the programme of a parliament'.[41] Finally, there were 'mind the shop' conservatives, who mostly resisted change or who made no more change than was absolutely necessary to preserve the society and institutions that they valued. Lord Salisbury seems to have been a conservative of this hue. Another possible exemplar of this type of conservatism is the group calling itself 'conservatives for an Australian head of state', claiming (mistakenly, in my view) that it was necessary to support the 1999 referendum proposal in order to preserve Australia's system of government from a subsequent more radical republic.

John Howard sometimes described himself as a 'Burkean conservative' (for instance, at the National Press Club on 11 September 2002). Revealingly, he has also referred to himself as a 'Burkean liberal' (in an address to the Tasmanian state council of the Liberal Party on 23 August 1997), quite legitimately, as the Whig statesman would have perfectly understood Tennyson's paradox of 'freedom broadening slowly down from precedent to precedent'. On at least two occasions, Howard invoked Burke's lovely metaphor of society as a 'partnership between the living, the dead and the yet unborn'. He also referred to Burke's notion of the 'little platoons' that make up the social fabric of functioning civil societies.

It's no slight on Howard to observe that he was not a systematic philosopher, because conservatism is not a systematic philosophy. Unlike liberalism or socialism, conservatism does not start with an idea and construct a huge superstructure based on one insight or preference. Conservatism starts with an appreciation of what is and what has been and tries to discern the good from patterns of conduct. Conservatism prefers facts to theory; practical demonstration to metaphysical abstraction; what works to what's in the mind's eye. To a conservative, intuition is as important as reasoning; instinct as important as intellect. A way of life has far more demonstrative power to a conservative than a brilliant argument. Conservatives are not optimists or pessimists but realists. They have a proper appreciation of the strengths of society as well as its individual and collective capacity for folly. They have an understanding of the need to get things right but also an appreciation of how easily this can go wrong.

Conservatism is not so much inarticulate as conscious of the limitations of all philosophies. The conservative appreciates that judgment is essentially provisional, wisdom relative, and success transient. That's why conservatives are often reluctant to pick fights although doughty once battle has been joined. They are better suited to defending barricades than to storming them. In this sense, conservatism may be less immediately exhilarating than other political positions, but it's no less deeply felt. It should be less self-righteous, but it's no less concerned with moral values and no less determined to do the right thing as conservatives are given to understand it.

Oakeshott thinks that, paradoxically, it could be the profound streak of conservatism in English-speaking societies that has enabled them to change so much so peacefully and to have maintained for so long a creative edge over other cultures. Change is relatively easy when few principles are dogmatically held and one person's opinion is considered as likely as the next person's to be right. It stands to reason that a society habituated to incremental change should find change less frightening and divisive. A political conservative normally only changes what has to be changed, makes the change conform as far as possible to established principles, and afterwards maintains that nothing much has really changed at all. By insisting that what's constant far outweighs what's changed and by constantly stressing unity over diversity, the conservative usually tries to make change as close to seamless and painless as it can be. It's no accident that Australia's most conservative recent prime minister has successfully presided over the biggest policy changes (workplace, welfare, and border protection reforms, for instance, and a much more assertive foreign policy), and the allegedly dullest and most conformist prime minister has best reconciled Australians to the diversity of their society.

John Howard frequently characterised his government as animated by 'mainstream values'. This was a shorthand way of saying that the government opposed change that was not in accordance with the best values and most characteristic behaviour of the Australian people but supported change that was. As prime minister, contrary to Hayek's contention, he demonstrated that conservatives could be vigorous reformers themselves rather than mere obstacles to obstruct the reforms of others.

An examination of the Howard Government's 'signature' policies shows deep concern for personal responsibility, individual choice, reward for effort, the protection of families, and respect for traditional institutions and time-honoured values. The government didn't self-consciously start with a set of values, though, and build a political plan around them. Rather, it looked at specific problems and devised policies to deal with them. These invariably turned out to reflect the values that the prime minister and his colleagues thought were the most broadly based in Australian society. The Howard Government certainly had a 'preference for freedom' that made it a 'liberal' government. Freedom, though, was but 'first among equals', so to speak, in the ranks of the government's principal political values, and often enough had to defer to one or more of the others.

It's hard to imagine the Howard Government's leading figures even entering parliament merely to exercise power. Strong conceptions of right and wrong underpinned all its policies. Still, this is quite different from being 'ideological'. In the marrow of his bones, Howard understood the distinction between, on the one hand, finding and appreciating the values in which human society is steeped and, on the other, trying to apply a priori intellectual concepts to the real world. For Howard, context was crucial. Good government wasn't bringing abstract ideals to bear on the organisation of society. Rather, it was trying to encourage people and institutions to operate at their best.

When Howard talked about political ideas, he hardly ever invoked labels or philosophical concepts. Instead, he tried to express himself in the type of language that people might normally use when trying to explain why they did something. In one of his rare 'academic' speeches, he insisted that there was no particular tension between 'economic policy liberalisation' and 'modern conservatism in social policy' because they both shared 'important common values and objectives'. Both, he said, rejected the corporate state, promoted opportunity and responsibility, and supported individual potential as well as social obligation. Both, he said, recognised 'the role of markets and of government as well as the limitations of each' and rejected 'the extremes of laissez-faire indifference to the social costs of economic change'.[42] In a 1998 Australia Day address, he quoted Francis Fukuyama's judgment that the principles beloved of economic liberals such as 'law, contract and economic rationality' depended upon the principles beloved of social conservatives such as 'reciprocity, moral obligation, duty towards community and trust which are based in habit rather than rational calculation'.

In seven years in the Howard cabinet, I cannot recall a single discussion canvassing a proposal's conformity with any kind of orthodoxy. Whether a proposal could be categorised as 'left-wing', 'right-wing', 'conservative', 'liberal', 'interventionist', 'deregulatory', 'capitalist', 'socialist', 'centralist' or 'federalist' didn't matter much compared with whether it might plausibly solve a problem in ways that would advance the national interest. That's why the 'ideological' tag that critics so often hung on him rarely struck a chord with voters. Howard's intention wasn't to impose his values on voters. Rather, it was to try to discern their values and to find solutions to problems based on them. As long as voters could see the common sense in the former government's proposals, the government prospered politically. This only changed when, with Work Choices, policy seemed to have become a solution in search of a problem.

Critics such as Robert Manne, who claim that the government's polices involved the conscious application of 'neo-liberal' or 'neo-conservative' ideology to economic or national-security problems, completely miss the point. A political party has to market its policies to voters, not philosophers. A politician wants to impress the electorate, not the political-science profession. Manne and others might discern in 'neo' ideology a profound explanation of the Howard Government's actions. If, in fact, the government was ever, in Keynes' sense, slave to long-dead philosophers, they would have been a pretty eclectic bunch. To the best of my awareness, not a single Howard cabinet member ever had any 'neo-ism' in mind when actually making a decision. To have made a decision based on abstract ideology would have been completely foreign to the government's whole way of working. Any decision made on such a basis would have been utterly unintelligible to the electorate. It's very hard to see how the government could have been re-elected three times if it really had been as ideologically programmed as Manne suggests.

For all his personal conservatism, Howard always insisted that a political party that wanted to win government had to have a broad-based political philosophy. To win elections, parties need policies that strike chords with voters, not with theorists. Hence, it's the actual appeal that parties make to voters, not the after-the-event tags applied by academics, that should be taken as best characterising a party's approach. The Howard Government had a preference for market mechanisms because these are generally most conducive to maximising choice. It usually supported US foreign policy measures (without being starry-eyed about their prospects) because it made sense to prefer liberal democracy to fundamentalism. It supported a goods and services tax, as a replacement for a range of other, less efficient taxes, because it spread the tax burden from earning to spending. It supported Work for the Dole because young unemployed people, in particular, should not be encouraged to expect something for nothing. The government supported workplace deregulation because it would make people easier to employ. It ramped up border protection because a country that doesn't control its borders is vulnerable to peaceful invasion. It supported the NT intervention because law and order is a prerequisite for a decent community. It gave a military commitment to East Timor and to failing Pacific island states because that's what a self-respecting regional power should have done. With eyes wide open, the government committed Australian forces to Afghanistan and Iraq because that's what being a reliable ally means.

A 'liberal' case could be made for all these policies. Tax reform was about 'lower, simpler taxes'; Work for the Dole was to demonstrate what people could do, not what they couldn't; workplace reform meant more freedom for workers and managers; border protection freed people from the oppression of people smuggling; the intervention empowered Aboriginal people to reclaim their lives; and Australian military forces went abroad in support of freedom from corruption and dictatorship.

Similarly, a 'conservative' case could be made. The GST gave the states access to a growth tax. Work for the Dole forced people to give something back to society. Workplace change reduced the power of interfering tribunals. Turning back boats was an assertion of Australian sovereignty. The intervention applied general community standards to Aboriginal townships. Australia's military forces were defending Western civilisation against the forces of chaos. Voters, I suspect, weren't much interested in whether these policies were properly considered as 'liberal' or 'conservative' as long as they struck some responsive chord and generally seemed to work.

In supporting the monarchy and articulating traditional family values, Howard was conservative. In cutting taxes and deregulating the labour market, he was liberal. In funding the Darwin–Alice Springs railway line and negotiating a free trade deal with America, he was pragmatic. In banning semi-automatic weapons and launching the emergency intervention in the Northern Territory, he seized opportunities, but it was an opportunism based on values. Essentially, he was an inspired pragmatist. The test he applied was: 'How could any particular measure help to make Australia a freer, stronger, better nation?' Ultimately, it was this sort of national-interest test that determined how Howard judged every proposal.

The former prime minister's attempts to put his government's policy into a coherent philosophical framework were rarely entirely convincing, because they tried to fit policies into straightforward categories when they were mostly complex responses to messy human situations and, at different times and to a different extent, drew on a range of important values. How necessary or important is it to be able to offer all-embracing explanations anyway? So far, the only one to try to offer a comprehensive explanation of the former government's policies is Kevin Rudd, who has attributed them all to 'market fundamentalism'. The fact that he tarred all recent governments with the same brush makes this attempt not merely implausible but laughable.

Perhaps it's enough to say that in some circumstances freedom and in other circumstances a set of rules is the most effective way to encourage people to be their best selves. Howard perhaps came closest to describing what the government was actually trying to do in a speech from 2000. There was, he said, 'a correlation between the principles, the priorities and the aspirations that Australians carry within themselves ... and the policy development framework of their national government'. In this speech he nominated 'self-reliance', 'a fair go', 'pulling together' and 'having a go' as elements of the 'Australian Way'.[43] This was the essence of Howard's approach. He tried to assimilate the values that he thought were at the heart of Australia. His political program was liberal to the extent that he thought Australians wanted to get on with their own lives, but it was conservative in its emphasis on the source and 'mainstream' content of those values.

Despite once describing himself as 'the most conservative leader the Liberal Party has ever had'[44], in his second stint as leader, he typically put an adjective in front of conservatism or talked about conservatism without actually describing himself as a conservative. He'd learnt from bitter experience not to make unnecessary enemies. In Australia, conservatism has tended to be the political orientation that dare not speak its name. As Abjorensen put it, for many years 'the 'c' word was simply not used in polite Liberal company'.[45] By so frequently invoking conservatism, however, Howard has confirmed that it's now a respectable political orientation in this country.

The antecedents of today's Liberal Party are the original Liberal Party, which Deakin fused together from 'conservative' free traders and 'liberal' protectionists; the Nationalist Party, amalgamating the Liberals with pro-conscription Labor MPs; and the United Australia Party, amalgamating the Nationalists with economically conservative Labor MPs. Menzies' Liberal Party was formed in 1944 by representatives of the Democratic Party, the Liberal Democratic Party, the Country National Organisation, the Queensland People's Party, the Queensland Women's Electoral League, the United Australia Organisation, the Australian Women's National League, the Young Nationalist Organisation, the Services and Citizens Party, and the Liberal and Country League. From its beginning, the party has been Liberal in name but not just liberal in nature.

It's too early to know the fate of the new Liberal National Party in Queensland, which is now the Queensland division of the Liberal Party of Australia (just as, for many years, the Liberal and Country League was its SA division). If the next Queensland election is contested by a credible leader from the former Liberal wing there is every chance that it could flourish, much as the Liberal and County League did. Especially if there is a risk of significant tension inside the coalition in Canberra, there could be a strong case for a merged party at the national level. 'Liberal National' might actually be a better description of the party's overall orientation than simply 'Liberal'. A merged party would be 'liberal' in its instinctive support for individual and community solutions over government ones and 'national' in its determination that Australia should matter in the wider world. 'Liberal' implies a particular philosophical orientation. 'National' implies a commitment to the country that transcends political ideology. As its record under John Howard shows, the Liberal Party certainly does have a preference for freedom, but it is, above all, a 'strong Australia' party.

What, now, needs to be done to make Australia stronger and truer to its best ideals? How can Australians individually and collectively come closer to being their 'best selves' and what can the Liberal Party do to bring this about? These are the questions that the rest of this book tries to probe.

4 Unfinished Business

I had been in parliament less than a year when I had my first fight over policy. It was over my 1995 proposal, in an article for *The Adelaide Review*, to restore Lake Pedder by draining the water stored behind the hydroelectric dam. Apparently, this attempt to burnish the party's environmental credentials had upset some senior Tasmanian Liberals. My next fight was over burying aerial cables, a proposal prompted by local opposition to the 1996 dual rollout of Telstra and Optus pay TV wiring on power poles. Before including me in the ministry in 1998, the prime minister stressed his 'Dutch uncle's' advice not to speak publicly outside my portfolio responsibilities.

As employment minister, I was in trouble for calling for a redesign of the tax-transfer system to reduce or eliminate poverty traps. As health minister, I was taken to task for urging consideration of a Commonwealth takeover of public hospitals. I was cautioned over my 2006 'new paternalism' speech, even though some of its ideas were reflected in the subsequent NT intervention. During the 2004 campaign, I earned a first-rate 'prime-ministerial bollocking', as a colleague once described such calls, for adding to the Medicare schedule (and thus to the safety net) a new item to cover the management of pregnancy. Still, I suspect that most policy rebukes were prompted more by the concerns of colleagues than by those of the prime minister himself.

Like all prime ministers, Howard preferred not to have his ministers flagging new policy initiatives that might make the government look ragged or divided. On the other hand, he also understood that the government's job is to make a difference. I suspect that he didn't really mind ministers canvassing new ideas, provided they reinforced the impression of a government concerned with mainstream values. He called me once, after reading a speculative news report, to enquire politely whether I was about to announce a royal commission into the construction industry, but was quite content when I said that this was only an idea that I wanted to discuss further. Howard knew in the marrow of his bones that effective government required a steady succession of innovative polices based on good values.

One of the handicaps that the conservative side of politics normally has to overcome is the popular impression that the Labor Party believes in fairness while the Liberal Party just believes in good economic management. In my experience, Liberals are hardly less passionate about fairness than members of the Labor Party. The key difference is Liberals' instinctive sense that a wealthier society is more likely to be fair than a poorer one. It's much easier to redistribute wealth to the needy if wealth is being created. Wealth creation means that there can be more for everyone rather than an ugly fight to take away what some people already have. In countries with market economies, successful Labor leaders have grasped this, too, but they invariably have had to resist the contrary instincts of their most passionate supporters. Labor leaders normally understand that 'soak the rich' policies can only be taken so far; but their followers often don't. Howard liked to quote Tony Blair's celebrated statement that 'fairness begins with the chance of a job' precisely because Britain's most successful Labour leader had used the phrase in an exasperated attempt to re-educate his own party.

The policies that the Howard Government immediately embarked upon in 1996 were designed to give Australia a stronger economy, not for merely its own sake but to create a society that was fairer and better realised its potential. Spending cuts, for instance, were pursued in order to allow lower taxes that would give more incentive to people who could create wealth. Workplace relations reform was needed so that workers could be more productive, businesses more profitable and wages higher. Of course, Labor politicians also want more wealth and higher wages. It's just that they tend to think, against the weight of recent evidence, that people will end up trying to exploit each other if left to their own devices. Following Hobbes, the ALP tends to think that government is necessary to prevent the war of all against all. Following Adam Smith, Liberals tend to think that government is necessary to keep the peace but otherwise should let people make mutually beneficial arrangements with each other. Deep down, the boringly pragmatic Liberal Party has a sunnier view of human nature than the passionately idealistic Labor Party because we are prepared to put more trust in the common sense and decency of our fellow Australians.

The economic reform that the Liberal Party often seems to be preoccupied with is about liberating people to be their best and most productive selves, not chaining them to the grinding wheels of production. A wealthier, more productive economy means more choice, more leisure and more opportunities for philanthropy. No amount of talk about social justice will deliver it if the economy is in free fall. That's why continued economic reform is more important than ever now that the economy is most likely in a prolonged slump.

The Howard Government started with the conviction that work wasn't an optional extra if the 'right' job was available. It thought that performing useful work was essential for most people's self-respect. Paradoxically, if a business could afford to let people go it could more readily afford to take them on and to pay them more. That was the whole point of workplace relations reform. Welfare reform was designed to ensure that people were encouraged to work and tax reform was designed to ensure that people had more incentive to earn. Some of these reforms had much further to go. One, notably, went too far. Together, they made Australia much stronger economically and were as important as the worldwide boom and good macro-economic management in driving the prosperity of the Howard era. Still, even after eleven years of sustained effort to reinforce a culture of enterprise and opportunity there was much more to be done.

In three important respects, the Rudd Government is already undermining this legacy: first, it's changing the workplace system to protect existing workers ahead of would-be workers and their employers; second, under the banner of 'compassion', it's reducing incentives to work; and third, as part of 'cutting middle-class welfare' it's removing benefits from the so-called aspirational classes, who are crucial to generating spending and creating employment in small business.

In many areas, the Rudd Government is repeating the mistakes of the Hawke and Keating Governments, only without the big reforms that redeemed the economic record of its Labor predecessors. The need for economic reform doesn't go away because a country is enjoying a boom or, for that matter, a recession. Opportunities to improve the way our businesses operate and our economy functions can never be neglected if our future prosperity is to be secured.

During the long boom, a magic-pudding mentality eventually took hold. People started to expect simultaneous tax cuts, spending increases and bigger surpluses as if these were part of the natural order of things rather than the unique product of sustained economic reform and a worldwide boom. Since the onset of the downturn, public debate has focused on recession-busting rather than the structural improvements that will make a lasting difference to our economy. It's been very hard to discern, as complacency became panic in the wake of the global financial crisis, much serious thinking about the next generation of economic reforms.

Some of these reforms won't seem like economic ones. Because a strong economy requires highly educated people in good health, better schools and hospitals, and better systems for running them, are an important component of economic reform. Because successful businesses require good infrastructure, better roads and telecommunications, and more effective ways to produce them, are also part of economic reform. Still, the foundation of a strong economy is competitive markets. After the maintenance of external and internal security, the key task of government is to create and preserve the circumstances in which markets can flourish. People and businesses need to be able to produce their goods and sell their services without unreasonable restrictions.

Australia's contemporary economic strengths are largely the result of the reforms undertaken by the past two governments. The Hawke/Keating Government deregulated financial markets, reduced tariffs and began the process of privatising government business assets. The Howard Government deregulated the labour market, significantly reformed the tax system and began the process of welfare reform to give more people more incentive to work. The cumulative effect of these changes was to help produce the largest, fastest and most widespread growth in prosperity in our history. During the Howard years, real wages increased by over 20 per cent, there were 2.2 million new jobs, and real net wealth per head more than doubled. When all forms of income are taken into account, the rich got richer and the poor got richer at a slightly faster rate.

Even so, reform is rarely popular or easy. Although the then opposition generally supported the Hawke Government's reforms, which, therefore, did not become big political problems, the Labor Party ferociously opposed nearly all the reforms of the Howard Government. Trying to justify Work Choices, John Howard in vain insisted that tomorrow's prosperity is based on today's reform. Instead, the general public questioned the need for further reform at a time when the economy was performing so well. Rather than reassuring voters that it was still 'on the job', the former government's fourth-term economic reforms (which included finally privatising Telstra and encouraging people on incapacity benefits to return to the workforce, in addition to further workplace change) were taken as proof that the government had become arrogant and out of touch.

There is very little evidence that the new government plans serious reforms other than, perhaps, an attack that's likely to backfire on so-called 'middle-class welfare'. Its most significant change so far has been to undo not only the Howard Government's labour-market reforms but those of the Keating Government too. There has been a big rise in union activity, strikes have more than doubled (admittedly off a very low base) and the new industrial legislation virtually compels business to manage its workforce in partnership with unions. The government's other policy innovation, an emissions trading scheme, amounts to a carbon tax flowing through to almost every sector of the economy. The Rudd Government has committed extra funds to schools and hospitals, but there's been no change to the way the states run their health and education institutions, so there's little likelihood of much lasting improvement. The government has promised more money for productive infrastructure, but delivery depends upon state governments with a very poor record in delivering major projects on time and on budget. The government has instituted numerous policy studies, but these are unlikely to produce reform recommendations that will be politically palatable without massive extra spending.

So far, apart from means tests on the Baby Bonus, the Family Tax Benefit and the Childcare Benefit, and that proposed for the Private Health Insurance rebate (all of which will harm families striving to get ahead), the government's new measures have involved very substantial extra spending. Commonwealth spending is forecast to rise from 24 per cent to 29 per cent of GDP and real per capita government spending growth is tipped to rise from 1.9 per cent to 4.1 per cent a year thanks to a Whitlam-style spendathon. There is little long-term economic gain in this new spending and it's a very expensive way to ameliorate the recession. The $52 billion that the government has recently spent on stimulus packages that have, even on its own estimation, protected just 200,000 workers adds up to about $250,000 per job. The government's forecasts have unemployment rising to 8.5 per cent by the middle of 2010 despite these measures. The impact of reduced revenue and extra spending, though, will be budget deficits at over 3 per cent of GDP for the foreseeable future and gross Commonwealth debt shooting to triple the levels reached under the Keating Government.

The government's response to the looming recession has been both hyperactive and unimaginative. There's been almost nothing so far to reduce the cost of employing people, such as reductions in payroll tax or in superannuation levies for recession-hit businesses. There's been nothing for small business, such as extended time to pay tax or, as Malcolm Turnbull has suggested, the ability to obtain a refund of previous years' taxes against the current year's losses, even though this is where job losses (and gains) will most quickly occur. Even though the main problem is failure to lend and invest, the government doesn't appear to have considered, for instance, dropping capital gains tax on new investment. The government doesn't seem to have noticed that, across the Tasman, the recently elected Key Government has reduced tax penalties and eased environmental-approval processes in an effort to help business.

Most recent recessions occurred because monetary authorities had raised interest rates to reduce demand and to cut inflation. The cause of this recession was the collapse of an asset price bubble. The basic problem in this recession is not so much lack of spending (although spending has indeed dropped) but lack of confidence. Until confidence is restored, spending will remain stubbornly low. Cash handouts will largely be saved, not spent. Given that the asset price bubble was generated by unsustainable debt in the first place, debt-funded government spending is much more likely to sap confidence than to restore it, especially if the money is spent on the fiscal equivalent of sugar hits. Some problems demand considered thought rather than immediate 'decisive action'. If the government had been less preoccupied with the politics of avoiding a recession and more conscious of the fundamental principle of government, 'first, do no harm', its policy might have been quite different.

Almost certainly, the economic slowdown will continue to reinforce the Labor Party's instinct for big government and more spending. Once the surpluses accumulated by its predecessor have run out, taxes will have to increase, interest rates will have to go up or inflation will rise, because the money has to come from somewhere. Almost certainly, the government will waste the opportunity this recession provides because it will be more reform-shy than usual just at the time when people are more inclined to contemplate the otherwise politically impossible. The government's addiction to 'decisive' but ill-thought-through action, though, could provide the opposition with the chance to display intellectual and policy leadership. Almost inevitably, the next coalition government will have to undertake a budget repair job at least comparable to Peter Costello's in 1996. In renewing the ongoing work of economic reform, it should also take on some of the challenges that the former government decided not to tackle. As well, it will have to revisit the workplace reforms that gave it so much political grief but that are central to a productive economy.

Work Choices Wasn't All Bad

Work Choices was a political mistake, but it may not have been an economic one. The legislation was highly complex, for all the government's deregulatory intent. Its chief fault, though, was to abolish the 'no disadvantage rule' that had previously applied to Australian Workplace Agreements. As John Stone has pointed out, during the 18-month period it was fully operational '499,000 jobs were added, of which 91 per cent were full time (compared to only 51 per cent during the preceding decade, when the Keating government's unfair-dismissals regime remained in full swing)'.[1] Thus, says Stone, while the measure was politically 'regrettable', 'it would be churlish to deny its remarkable success during its brief life in boosting Australia's labour market performance'.[2]

The new government has not just abolished Work Choices. It has largely scrapped the law that had operated since 1993, when the Keating Government enshrined enterprise bargaining in preference to arbitrated wage settlements. The new system requires businesses to engage in 'good-faith bargaining'—a coercive misnomer—with, potentially, all unions that have workers at an enterprise. A new industrial regulator-cum-arbiter, Fair Work Australia, is to make binding rulings in the event that the parties can't agree. This is compulsory arbitration by the back door. It means that decisions vital to the survival of businesses and their employees will be made by officials rather than by people in the workplace.

As Michael Costa said recently:

> the real problem with the [new] legislation is its model of collective bargaining ... The introduction of compulsory 'good faith' bargaining with a new arbitral body,

> Fair Work Australia, means that an effective broad re-regulation of the labour market is likely. This overturns not only Work Choices but also important reforms made in labour market regulation under the Hawke and Keating Labor governments.
>
> Good faith is extremely difficult to establish in practice and will result ... in more arbitrated outcomes. Industrial arbitration, by its nature, tries to please everybody and quite often, as a result, pleases nobody ... Workplace productivity could suffer ...
>
> Fair Work Australia cannot be allowed to replace enterprise management in developing business strategy. This would be an unmitigated economic disaster.[3]

This is by far the most destructive element in the new legislation. The much-touted abolition of Australian Workplace Agreements could be relatively insignificant by comparison, especially as there is provision for workers on awards to be put on contracts that will not be further tested against the award provided they satisfy Fair Work Australia that people on them will be 'better off all round'. The continuing need for contracts outside the award system is demonstrated by the fact that 90,000 transitional employment agreements have already been created under the new government's legislation. Despite its popularity, though, the new government's version of an AWA will no longer be available after 2010. The type of statutory employment contract that the ALP regards as fair, even if only for the time being, ought to be available on an ongoing basis. It's hard to imagine how the ALP or the union movement could successfully demonise, if proposed by the coalition, a type of contract that its own legislation had originally created.

On more than forty separate occasions, prior to the 2004 election, the Howard Government tried to pass laws exempting small business from unfair dismissal provisions. Businesses with fewer than twenty full-time employees are more like a family than an institution. If someone doesn't fit in, it's best that he or she goes. It's not fair to other workers to put the future of the business at risk by insisting that people have to be expensively paid off or kept on until they've more than proven they're not suitable. The profitability of small business is precarious enough without being saddled with dud workers or big payouts, and the policy of the next coalition government should recognise this.

As well, it will be important for a future coalition government to restore the rule of law in the commercial construction sector, otherwise it will be subject, as the Cole royal commission and the subsequent Wilcox inquiry demonstrated, to widespread industrial intimidation. The Master Builders' Association has commissioned research to show that the establishment of the Australian Building and Construction Commission (which the Rudd Government has pledged to abolish) has boosted productivity by at least 10 per cent, providing a $5-billion-a-year boost to the economy. The new government says it will keep a 'cop on the beat' but proposes to do this through Fair Work Australia, notwithstanding the industrial relations system's culture of conciliating law breakers rather than punishing them. This would all-but-guarantee the return of stand-over tactics to a historically troubled industry, jeopardising investment and jobs.

It's not surprising that the Rudd Government is slowly turning Work for the Dole into a training program. The idea that 'the world owes people a living' is strong inside the Labor Party. This is why even a normally sensible frontbencher like Martin Ferguson once called Work for the Dole 'almost evil'. The Labor Party is also eroding the principle of mutual obligation. Although the former government's 'three strikes and you're off benefit' rule may not have been readily enforceable, there's little reason to think that the new government's suspension of benefit for 'no-shows' at job interviews and training programs is going to be rigorously enforced either. As well, the reduction of benefit taper rates for disability pensioners will reduce their incentive to work.

Although most people don't choose to be on welfare, once they've become accustomed to it, it's easy enough to find reasons why going back to work is too hard. Activity testing, especially participation in Work for the Dole, needs to become more routine, not less. People need to begin Work for the Dole sooner, not later than was the case under the Howard Government, and stay on it until they've found work or moved onto a different benefit. After a month on benefit, people should participate in job-search training, and after three months they should begin regular Work for the Dole. Especially in a recession, with unemployment rising sharply, it's important to keep people connected to the labour market and in structured activity on days they're not looking for work.

Social Security Shouldn't Be Forever

One of the former government's significant achievements was slowing the rise in the number of people claiming the disability pension. In many cases, going on the disability pension was a form of disguised unemployment. The former government introduced more rigorous medical examinations, often conducted by government doctors, and changed the disability pension's eligibility rule from incapacity to work almost full-time to incapacity for fifteen hours' work a week. The former government also imposed modest activity requirements on sole-parent pensioners, who were expected to attend a job-search interview once their youngest child went to school.

Even though the anti-government swing was higher in seats with significant welfare dependency, the coalition should not lightly abandon these sorts of policies. In bad times, voters are less likely to indulge people who could readily work but don't. Paradoxically, expecting more of people on welfare could seem less harsh with the budget in massive deficit than when the government appeared to have money to spare.

More use could be made of systems for assessing degrees of impairment and then expecting more of a disability pensioner with a bad back, for instance, than one who's paraplegic. 'Disability' covers an enormous range of conditions and there's plainly an argument for being less exacting towards the severely handicapped but more rigorous with people whose condition is comparatively slight, not necessarily permanent or a modest impediment at most to many types of employment.

Another important reform would be generally subjecting welfare-dependent families with children under sixteen to automatic income management, not just those in the remote towns of the Northern Territory. Since 50 per cent of welfare income has been quarantined to the necessities of life, local women and officials report less drunkenness, better nourishment and, in some cases, higher school attendance. Some people in other remote welfare-dependent towns have asked for Territory-style controls. There are welfare neighbourhoods in outer metropolitan areas and regional towns with social problems not unlike those of the Territory. Endemic substance abuse and family violence are not an Aboriginal issue. They're the all-but-inevitable result of too many people with not enough to do, regardless of race or culture.

Welfare quarantine is not a panacea, but it does make it much harder for taxpayer-provided funds to be misused. Of course, in the Territory, as elsewhere, there are many families who spend their money responsibly. These families would already spend well over 50 per cent of their welfare income on the necessities of life, so they should not be affected or inconvenienced by such a change. For other families, as in the Territory, there would be at least some food on the table and more possibility of saving for household goods. General welfare quarantine, at least for welfare-dependent families with children, would send the clearest possible message that people on welfare have obligations as well as entitlements.

Maintaining high expectations of people on welfare is an important economic reform in two respects: first, it is likely to keep the welfare bill as low as possible; and second, it helps to maximise the number of people actually in work and part of the productive economy. In this area, the former government understood what many economists were inclined to ignore: namely, the impact of welfare on people's willingness to take work.

It's not just the availability of work but its rewards that matter to people on welfare. Standard economic concepts such as a 'market-clearing wage' don't apply when the alternative to working is life on welfare. Contrary to the economic textbook, lower wages don't boost employment if the people who might earn them don't have to work. This helps to explain why unemployment remained stubbornly high throughout the life of the Hawke and Keating Governments, even though wages hardly grew in thirteen years. It also helps to explain why unemployment is 'sticky' even in the face of the kind of labour shortages that developed in the second half of the Howard Government's term.

In the employment portfolio between 1998 and 2003, one of my main missions was to highlight the importance of improving incentives to work, sometimes to the irritation of colleagues on whose portfolios I was trespassing. In many speeches from this period (for instance, to the Young Liberals in 2003), I pointed out the high effective marginal tax rates faced by people moving from welfare to work.

As employment minister, I was responsible for spending over $1 billion a year to help people to find jobs that, thanks to the perverse interaction of the tax and social-security systems, would often leave them virtually no better off. The Job Network was striving to find employment for people, while the means-tested social-security system all too often meant that taking a job was more trouble than it was worth. For many people on welfare, taking a $12-a-hour job—that was really a $4-an-hour job once tax was paid and benefits were lost—was hardly worth the bother.

To its credit, the Howard Government subsequently addressed these disincentives to work by cutting taxes on low incomes and further reducing the withdrawal rate at which most benefits decline as income increases. These changes meant that many people moving from welfare to work kept much more of their earned income. However, reducing the clawback rate meant that more people were eligible for benefits and therefore subject to both income tax and benefit withdrawal whenever their income increased. As a result, during the life of the Howard Government, the percentage of people facing effective marginal tax rates above 50 per cent actually increased from 4 per cent to 8 per cent.

The Trouble with Means Tests

The basic problem, as I kept pointing out during my time in the employment portfolio, is the means test. Because they reduce the benefit of moving from welfare to work, means tests designed to ensure that only the needy receive government benefits can have the perverse impact of keeping people poor. 'The interaction of a needs-based, highly targeted welfare system with a progressive tax system', I said in 2003, 'becomes even more complex for low- to middle-income families receiving multiple benefits (with cumulative and often different thresholds and withdrawal rates). For families, the worst poverty traps can occur when moving from low to middle levels of earned income.' It was then the case that, depending on its circumstances, a family earning an extra $300 a week could actually be worse off.

In 1994, in my maiden speech to parliament, I had described middle-income families with children as Australia's new poor and called for a (non–means tested) family wage, perhaps of $100 a week, to be paid to the principal carer of dependent children. A family wage, I said:

> is quite different from welfare. It is a recognition of responsibilities, not need. It is a payment for services, not a handout. It means that personal choice could replace economic necessity as a rationale for family decisions. One beauty of a family wage system, unlike a tax rebate, is that it would take one public servant, just one, and a computer to administer. Payments could start the moment a birth is recorded on the Registrar of Births, Deaths and Marriages database and finish 16 years later.

Being against 'middle-class welfare' makes an easy slogan but, like so many seemingly good ideas in public policy, it turns out to have serious unintended consequences. A means test is absolutely necessary if benefits are to be targeted to people most in need. The consequence of a means test, though, is that relatively poor people who earn an extra dollar can both lose benefit and pay tax at an effective rate that highly paid executives would consider a serious disincentive to work. With means tests, all that can change is the level of income at which poverty traps exist. In this way, the well-intentioned elimination of 'middle-class welfare' can readily condemn people to high effective marginal tax rates and consequent poverty traps. This is just what means tests unavoidably do, especially multiple means tests all applied with the worthy intention of ensuring that benefits are 'carefully targeted'.

The Rudd Government's attack on 'middle-class welfare' is, of course, full of double standards: why, for instance, is the private health insurance rebate middle-class welfare to be means tested but the childcare rebate not? In fact, both are meant to encourage important public-policy goals: maximising private contributions to health care and facilitating the workforce participation of women with children. The means test ensures that people are penalised just as they start to achieve. It's right that people who can't (and even a few who won't) provide for themselves receive support. But should they be the only people that government helps, especially when the means tests to make this happen can so easily produce a ladder of success with a few rungs missing? A system where every government payment is regarded pejoratively as 'welfare' to be rigorously means tested ends up subsidising need and, perversely, risks producing more of it. The selectivity of Labor's means tests—on 'aspirational' benefits but not on 'women's' ones—gives the game away. These changes are about helping Labor's constituencies rather than reforming the economy.

It's now clear that Kevin Rudd is running a very traditional Labor government. While his predecessors used previous recessions as an opportunity to drive reforms that were out of Labor character, the Rudd Government has used the current recession to revert to Labor type. This is a traditional borrow-and-spend Labor government that is exploiting the recession to justify increased spending on groups likely to vote Labor and using the deficit to justify removing benefits from families earning $150,000 a year as if they are all 'rich'.

The Howard Government's tax offsets and reductions to withdrawal rates reduced the severity of poverty traps and moved them higher up the income scale, where their disincentive effects should have been less. Still, a 2007 paper from the National Centre for Social and Economic Modelling revealed, paradoxically, that families on 150 per cent of average weekly earnings had much lower effective marginal tax rates than families on 50 per cent of average weekly earnings because of the much greater welfare benefits that low-income families receive. A 2008 Natsem paper revealed that 15.6 per cent of all families receiving Family Tax Benefit Part A currently face effective marginal tax rates above 50 per cent. Reducing the benefit withdrawal rate from 20 per cent to 10 per cent, however, would reduce the percentage of FTB(A) beneficiaries facing 50-per-cent-plus effective tax rates to just 6.7 per cent, at the cost of $1.7 billion a year.[4] Of course, eliminating the FTB(A) means test entirely would remove all the poverty traps associated with this particular benefit. It would be far better, at least for some benefits, to make them automatic entitlements rather than conditional welfare. Universal benefits create no poverty traps. Means testing family assistance, for instance, has had two pernicious impacts: the first is the denial to many families of any recognition of the costs of children; the second is the disincentives imposed on modest-income families moving from welfare into work or substantially increasing their earned income.

How Families Have Been Forgotten

Over time, means testing family benefits has significantly worsened the financial position of middle-income families, with far-reaching social and economic consequences. In a 2001 book, Barry Maley, a research fellow with the Centre for Independent Studies, outlined the history of government assistance to families with children. In the celebrated Harvester case of 1908, Justice Higgins declared that the Australian basic wage should be set at a level that would support a worker, his wife and two children in 'frugal comfort'. This promise of adequate financial support for families, whether through wages or through the social welfare system, was a key element in what Paul Kelly has called the 'Australian settlement'. To cope with the eroding value of the basic wage, in 1941, the Menzies Government introduced child endowment as a universal payment of equal value for all children regardless of family income. Support for families was maintained during the 1950s and '60s through the introduction of a range of tax deductions for dependent spouses and children. From the 1980s, though, family payments became means-tested welfare benefits rather than universal entitlements.

In 1960, said Maley, a single-income family comprising a couple and three dependent children on 150 per cent of average weekly earnings, 'after deductions and child allowances, paid no income tax and had a final disposable income 3 per cent above its earned income'. A comparable family in 2001, though, lost about 20 per cent of its earned income after taxation and family payments had been taken into account. Such a family, said Maley, was 23 per cent or nearly $14,000 a year worse off than its 1960 counterpart.[5] With government support rapidly tapering off once families with children earned more than average earnings, the central issue in family taxation, Maley said, was the 'unresolved problem of appropriate recognition of the unavoidable costs of raising children'.[6] Maley said that this was a crucial factor in the Australian birth rate falling from 3.5 in 1960 to 1.7 by 2001. He even linked the post-1960 growth in children born to unmarried mothers, from 5 per cent to 30 per cent of all births; sole-parent families, from 10 per cent to 25 per cent of total families; juvenile crime, up tenfold; and youth suicide, up fourfold, to this reduction in support for families with children.[7]

In launching the 2004 budget, Treasurer Peter Costello famously advised Australian parents to have at least three children: one for the mother, one for the father and one for the country. As Costello well understood, people don't start families in a vacuum. Their readiness to have children depends, in large measure, on their confidence in the security and prosperity of the family they might create. Improving the financial position of families with children was one of the clear objectives of the Howard Government. It's noteworthy that Australia enjoyed a significant up-tick in the birth rate, from 1.7 to 1.9, in the later years of the Howard Government, especially after the start of significant Baby Bonus payments in 2005.

The former treasurer's budget comments caused such a stir because it had been so rare for modern Australian governments to talk about the need for more children. Perhaps talking up the birth rate was subliminally associated with the days of 'populate or perish' and the spectre of being overrun by the 'yellow peril'. Perhaps it smacked of government interfering in the bedroom. In any event, one of the most important indicators of a country's confidence in itself had been officially overlooked for years.

The basic problem is that most Western countries have privatised the next generation. Having children tends to be regarded as a personal choice rather than a social good. Perhaps for the first time in human history, large families are seen not as a sign of faith in the future or even as provision against its perils but as a kind of trespass on the environment. As a consequence of these changing mores, government policies are no longer pitched to support families with children as a self-evident good but to households with low incomes judged therefore to be objectively in need. The financial position of middle-income families with children, especially those with one breadwinner, is dramatically worse than it was two generations ago. It's hardly surprising, under these circumstances, that middle-class Australian families are now mostly much smaller than they were.

Even a birth rate of 1.9 is well below the replacement rate. As Malcolm Turnbull declared in 2003, when he was Chairman of the Menzies Research Centre and treasurer of the Liberal Party, 'there is no greater threat to Western society than the decline in fertility … A society which cannot reproduce itself has surely embraced a cultural death wish'.[8]

The Child Drought

Supporting women who have children should be one of the important duties of government. Regardless of whether they are 'work-centred', 'home-centred' or 'adaptive', to use the British sociologist Catherine Hakim's characterisations, most women want to have children. At present, through the provision of substantial welfare benefits, government policy supports low-income mothers. Through the provision of significant childcare benefits, government policy supports mothers in the paid workforce, especially full-time ones. What government policy does not currently do is provide help for women in middle-income families or for women taking time off work to have a baby. The result is that many women have fewer children than they would like.

What's missing is a universal system of family assistance to support 'home-centred' and 'adaptive' women who have more children and also a comprehensive maternity-leave system to support 'work-centred' mothers who want to have more children. These measures would complement the access to part-time work (which the former government's workplace changes made easier) for those mothers who also want a career outside the home or who simply need the extra money.

In her Menzies Research Centre study, Lucy Sullivan (like Maley, a research fellow with the CIS) compared and contrasted the impact of different government policies on women's fertility. She considered the international evidence from countries ranging from Sweden, with strong maternity-leave and childcare policies, to Spain, with few 'gender equity' programs. Her conclusion was that the crux of the low fertility problem is not that women prefer having a career to having a family but 'inadequate income to support a family'.[9] Sullivan observed that 'Childcare appeals mainly to work-centred women'. By contrast, she said, 'both adaptive and home-centred women prefer to look after their pre-school children themselves and disapprove of the lack of financial support for families during this period of heightened responsibility'.[10]

Sullivan noted that during the 1950s, when universal family assistance was at its most extensive, 'fertility in higher income groups began to outstrip that in lower income groups'.[11] Now, thanks in part to the support directed to low-income families, fertility is highest in the lowest three socio-economic deciles.[12] Fertility drops, though, for women in families with more than 75 per cent of average weekly earnings. These are the women, says Sullivan, 'most likely to be attempting to maintain family income by participation in part time work, who know that an additional child will exacerbate the no-win trade-off of mothering deprivation and sufficient family income'.[13]

Sullivan says that the number of children women have is very strongly influenced by their 'family lifestyle expectations'. She says that, over the past century, Western countries have only achieved replacement-level fertility 'for the whole population' in the 'period after World War II when family income support was universal'. Today, in countries like Australia, replacement-level fertility is only generally achieved for women in modest-income families where welfare incomes 'are similar to or better than they could achieve for themselves in employment or would receive if unemployed but without dependent children'.[14]

Sullivan thinks that a universal family payment is needed to ensure justice for women and to boost the birth rate. She cited the French and Norwegian experience, where the introduction of a 'mother's wage' had lifted fertility respectively from 1.7 to 1.9 and from 1.7 to 1.8.[15] The ANU demographer Peter McDonald has also argued that there needs to be more financial support for families with children and more support for women to combine motherhood with another career. He says that policy changes that would be more conducive to bigger families are 'both desirable and achievable'[16], and that the view that 'pro-natalist' policies are expensive and futile is 'curious … given the weight of evidence'.[17]

In a speech to the 2003 National Population Summit, Malcolm Turnbull said that Australia needed to pursue some clear national goals in the field of family policy. These should include:

> the promotion of pro-natalist policies designed to ensure that, ideally, our birth rate increases closer to the replacement level of 2.1 … the recognition that children are a social good and not merely a private, optional pleasure … [and] the recognition that there is nothing any of us are likely to do which is more important to the future of this nation than to bear and raise children.[18]

He said that policy makers should 'stop being obsessed with hang-ups about 'middle-class welfare' and take pro-active steps to make it easier for our most skilled women to have the children every survey tells us that they want to have but experience shows too many of them have been denied'. In particular, he said, 'we should seriously consider replacing what is a fairly complex system of child and childcare support with a single payment to each mother per child'. In principle, he asked, 'is there any reason why the state should spend differential amounts in respect of a child based on whether the mother of that child works full-time, part-time or cares for the child at home?'[19]

Turnbull endorsed for 'careful consideration' a proposal for a new tax-free payment to all mothers set near the maximum level of Family Tax Benefit. 'I wonder', he said:

> whether the critics of increased family support are not missing the point. Just as increased military expenditure is something we must shoulder to meet the threat of terrorism, so is increased family support a necessary burden if we are to meet the threat of declining fertility.[20]

This speech reveals a conservative side to Turnbull's political character, quite different to 'Wentworth man', and may be an important guide to the instincts that would shape a Turnbull government.

For many families receiving Family Tax Benefit, it could be considered a reimbursement of tax rather than 'middle-class welfare'. The Howard Government tried to make this point by allowing families to claim their FTB through the tax rather than through the social security system. Although very few families did actually claim FTB by way of reduced Pay As You Go tax instalments, allowing the option was a way to demonstrate that it was more a family tax cut than just another government payment.

A Fair Go for Working Mothers

As Turnbull recognised in this speech, it's not enough to give more support to families once they have children. Women also need support in their initial choice to become mothers. Because women are normally in the workforce before they have children, this means the provision of effective maternity leave. People in the workforce can't normally forgo their income, even temporarily, without careful planning and a great deal of preparation. For mothers-to-be, there's not only the need to maintain income but also the natural instinct to be with their babies at least for the first few months of their lives.

The Howard Government did much to support women's choice. It tripled spending on child care and doubled the number of child-care places available. More flexible workplace arrangements made it easier for mothers to choose to work part-time or to have family-friendly hours. Under the Howard Government, the participation rate for women aged twenty to forty-nine rose from 66 per cent to 71 per cent, and for lone-parent women with dependent children from 40 per cent to 52 per cent.[21] One challenge that the former government inadequately met, though, was the establishment of a national maternity-leave scheme.

This was a difficult nettle for the former government to grasp. It encouraged businesses to provide some form of paid maternity leave (the Productivity Commission says that 53 per cent of women in the workforce have access to it) but was consistently reluctant to go further. Requiring individual businesses to offer paid maternity leave would have made younger women less employable. On the other hand, a taxpayer-funded paid-maternity-leave scheme (including the one that the Productivity Commission recommended) would have discriminated against mothers who weren't in the paid workforce. In part, the Baby Bonus was conceived as a way to resolve this dilemma.

Cabinet saw the Baby Bonus as a form of maternity leave for women in the paid workforce and also as recognition for all mothers of the cost of having children. It was set at $5000 because that was more or less the value of twelve weeks' pay at the then minimum award rate. To women's groups, however, it could not be considered maternity leave, precisely because it was a universal payment. To count as maternity leave, it had to be a benefit provided only to women in the paid workforce. The right to time off to have children, they said, should be as much a normal condition of employment as time off to recover from illness or for holidays.

The Rudd Government's proposed parental leave scheme is only for women in the paid workforce, but it's not funded by business as, by rights, it should be. At eighteen weeks, it's not long enough to allow women fully to breast-feed their babies and, at the level of the minimum award wage, it's inadequate for most families that depend on a mother's income. In some cases, accessing the $9700 taxed maternity leave payment will leave women worse off than they would be with their existing untaxed baby bonus and family tax benefits. The scheme was a last-minute budget bolt-on (as its absence from the forward estimates shows), designed so the government could claim a 'historic' first, rather than a serious attempt to make a difference for working mums.

If business is expected not only to cover employees' time off for sickness and personal leave but also to contribute to their retirement income, it's not unreasonable to expect it also to bear the cost of providing modest maternity leave. It could be funded through a small general levy (similar to the super levy), because requiring individual businesses to carry the specific maternity costs of each of their female employees could cause some employers to think twice about hiring women. Small business would instinctively regard any extra cost as unfair (as it would be while the recession lasts) but could perhaps be mollified by other measures to help, such as restoring their exemption from unfair dismissal laws or cutting the payroll tax rate or the company tax rate to 'make room' for a maternity leave levy.

The recent report of the Productivity Commission estimated that the cost of providing women in the paid workforce with eighteen weeks' maternity leave at the minimum award rate would be about 0.3 per cent of total payroll. A 0.5 per cent payroll levy on all business would remove any motivation to overlook potential women employees while funding up to six months' pay for new mothers. Six months is the recommended minimum time for babies to be exclusively breast-fed. In its submission to the Productivity Commission, the National Foundation for Women recommended a six months' paid maternity leave scheme that would replace a mother's full wages. The $4.4-billion-a-year cost should be funded, the foundation said, by a 0.75 per cent levy on payroll to create a pool of funds from which leave would be paid.

In the end, a paid maternity leave scheme, like more support for families with children, is a matter of fairness as well as a likely boost to fertility. Anything that makes having children easier is likely to mean more of them. Women in the paid workforce generally have fewer children than those who are not. A paid maternity leave scheme could motivate some career women to choose to have a child and others to choose to have two children rather than just one. Inevitably, having children makes it harder for women to pursue a career with the single-mindedness of colleagues who have someone else to do some of their parenting. High achievers who would like to be mothers should not have extra obstacles put in their way. A national maternity leave scheme would not only make it easier to combine motherhood with a career outside the home. It would also send the very traditional message that motherhood is important for all women.

Conservatives have been ambivalent towards maternity-leave schemes lest they encourage women to forsake their traditional roles. What slowly changed my mind was the experience of female colleagues who often felt torn between the demands of parliamentary life and the duties of motherhood. As Jackie Kelly has most persistently argued, more support was needed if women were both to stay in the workforce and continue to have children. The parliamentary childcare centre, for instance, which she did so much to bring about, was absolutely necessary if conservative, motherhood-minded women were to enter parliament before their children had grown up.

Given that nearly 60 per cent of women are in paid employment just before they become mothers and that 30 per cent of previously employed mothers are back at work within six months of having a baby[22], maternity-leave schemes are better thought of as a means of encouraging more women to keep the most traditional role of all: that of mother. Sullivan cited a UK survey that found 81 per cent of pregnant women and mothers with infants would give up work if they could. It's the fact that so many mothers and mothers-to-be can't afford to give up work that makes a national paid maternity leave scheme necessary and arguably overdue.

A Stimulus Package for Families

Of course, providing even more support to families with children would be a big fiscal challenge in the short term and, depending upon how far a government decided to go, a huge political and policy challenge in the long term. An immediate symbolic step could be to remove the Rudd Government's Baby Bonus means test, which saves only 3 per cent of total program spending but which has turned this payment from a recognition of the costs of motherhood into a welfare measure.

Another relatively achievable change would be to remove the means test on Family Tax Benefit Part A. At present, the maximum rate of about $75 a week starts to reduce once family income exceeds about $43,000. This would benefit an extra million families with children (about a third of all families with children) who currently receive no FTB(A). It would also mean higher benefits for families currently receiving less than the maximum rate. If this were done, people bringing up children would receive a benefit based not on their need but on the contribution that they are making to Australia's future. It would be a very significant recognition of the importance of parenting and of the value of children and should, over time, have an appreciable impact on the birth rate.

The Parliamentary Library has estimated that abolishing the means test on FTB(A) for all children under five would cost just under $2 billion a year. Such a policy would produce no direct losers. The library has also estimated that the impact of bracket creep has produced 'in the order of $1.5 to $1.7 billion' a year in additional Commonwealth revenue. In other words, the proceeds of a single year's bracket creep, let alone new spending of the magnitude now customary from the Rudd Government, could all but re-establish the first Menzies Government's principle that the main family benefit should be universal, not means tested.

In his parliamentary speech introducing the 1941 Child Endowment Bill, the then Minister for Labour and National Service,

Harold Holt, cited JM Keynes as an advocate of universal family allowances and quoted from his book, *How to Pay for the War*:

> At first sight it is paradoxical to propose in time of war an expensive social reform which we have not thought ourselves able to afford in time of peace. But in truth the need for this reform is so much greater in such times that it may provide the most appropriate occasion for it.[23]

A much bigger challenge would be rebuilding the tax-transfer system to take into account people's responsibilities as well as their income. Such a change would have the potential not only to recognise better the costs of having children but also to reduce or even to eliminate the poverty traps with which the current system is riddled. There is clearly something odd about a system that puts money into one pocket while taking it out of another. This 'churn' arises whenever people who receive welfare payments are also subject to tax.

Ideally, welfare benefits would give households a minimum level of income. Beyond that, earned income would not be taxed up to a further level depending on household size. After that, earned income could be taxed but not at a rate likely to destroy incentive. Suppose, for instance, that welfare were to provide a single adult with $15,000 a year; a dependent adult with $10,000 a year; and a dependent child with $5000 a year. Under such a system, a household of two adults and two dependent children with no earned income would receive $35,000 a year from welfare. If welfare benefits were withdrawn at a rate (say) of 40 cents in the earned dollar, this household would only start paying tax once its combined earned income exceeded $88,000 a year, the level at which welfare benefits would cut out. The household would be treated as a single entity for the purposes of entitlement to welfare and liability for tax. Provided tax was only paid once all welfare entitlements had been exhausted, poverty traps would be eliminated. The Centre for Independent Studies' Professor Peter Saunders has canvassed a system of this type as a way of avoiding the problem of means tests, although he notes that there would be a 'substantial' cost in lost government revenue.[24]

In the real world, of course, families can receive a large number of welfare benefits (such as Family Tax Benefit Part A and Family Tax Benefit Part B, childcare assistance, rent assistance, and youth allowance for older dependent children, each with different means tests). As well, earned income is taxed progressively on an individual rather than on a household basis. Substituting one payment for a variety of payments targeted to particular circumstances would be a huge challenge. Tweaking such a system to avoid numerous losers or a horrendous cost to the revenue might be almost impossible. Under the former government, a public-service taskforce considered but did not further proceed with the comprehensive change needed to produce such a system. Instead, the Howard Government reduced the problem, without eliminating it, through lower tax rates, reduced withdrawal rates, low income tax offsets, and the introduction of new benefits such as the Baby Bonus that were not means tested at all.

Ideals cannot always be realised, at least in the short to medium term. Still, the goal of policy should be to move further towards a system where, in any particular family circumstances and at any level of income, individuals can earn more and keep a reasonable share of it.

Paying for Reform

One way to help pay for a universal benefit for dependent children (such as the abolition of the means test on Family Tax Benefit Part A) might be to raise further and more quickly the age of pension eligibility. The Intergenerational Report estimated that, by 2047, there would be just 2.4 workers (rather than five as there are now) for every retired person, with an associated $35 billion 'fiscal gap'.[25] This assumed that Australians would continue to retire at about sixty-three for men and sixty for women, but why should they?

The Rudd Government's decision to lift the pension age to sixty-seven by 2023 should start a debate about older workers, not finish it. In Australia, eligibility for the old-age pension at sixty-five was introduced in the early 1900s, when life expectancy at birth was under sixty.

Today, life expectancy at birth is over eighty. In 1908, male life expectancy at sixty-five was 11.3 years. Today, it's 18.1 years.[26] A comparable pension age today would be at least seventy, especially as people in their sixties generally enjoy better health than their forebears a century ago. It's noteworthy that the Harmer report, on which the government's pension eligibility increase was based, recommended an increase of two to four years (or up to sixty-nine). Over the next forty years, male life expectancy at sixty is forecast to rise by another three years. Why should Australians continue to expect to retire on the old-age pension at sixty-five or even at sixty-seven, especially when the pool of younger workers to pay for them is shrinking as a percentage of the population? Without a significant increase in the birth rate, a big increase in the productivity of the workforce or, perish the thought, a decline in life expectancy, raising the age at which people retire is the only way to overcome the demographic destiny that the Intergenerational Report has highlighted.

The Howard Government took a number of measures to encourage people to work longer. There was the deferred pension plan that gave pension-eligible people working until seventy a lump-sum bonus of up to $33,000. There were changes to superannuation that made it much more worthwhile to work for longer beyond fifty-five. It never contemplated, though, raising the age of pension eligibility, even though this might be the most effective way to keep older Australians working.

Depending on their job, their health, their interests and their finances, many Australians are happy to leave the workforce at sixty-five or earlier. Others, though, resent being thought 'past it' at sixty-five and would be quite happy to keep working because they enjoy their jobs or want to be better off. Raising the pension age should change society's expectations about people's capacity for work. It should push back the age at which people are thought to be beyond their use-by date.

After New Zealand raised the pension age from sixty to sixty-five in the 1990s, participation rates for people aged fifty-five to sixty-four increased by 15 percentage points.[27] In the United States, where there are no means tests for age pensioners and thus no disincentives to keep working, 30 per cent of people aged sixty-five to sixty-nine still work, compared to only 18 per cent in Australia.

Of course, further raising the pension age would not stop people from retiring earlier if they could support themselves. It would not stop people from leaving the workforce on a disability pension if they were no longer capable of sustained work. In fact, about 80 per cent of people who move onto the full age pension do so from other benefits. This is why the savings from pension eligibility even at seventy would be relatively modest (a CEDA paper estimated the savings from raising the pension age to sixty-seven at perhaps $800 million a year). In practice, raising the pension age should leave few conscripts in the workforce but would make it much easier for older people who want to keep their jobs to do so.

Before they claim the pension, retirees are supposed to read and understand a 25-page Centrelink booklet and then complete three quite complex forms: respectively twenty-seven pages, twenty-two pages and twenty-four pages. Question A2 on the income and assets form requires claimants to estimate the market value of their household contents and personal effects. Strictly speaking, pensioners and part-pensioners with personal effects for which there is a clear market value should adjust this information in line with price movements. For strict compliance with social security law, gold jewellery, for instance, should be revalued in line with changes in the gold price. The fact that this is neither feasible nor readily expected illustrates another problem with means tests.

The cost of superannuation concessions is another issue to consider. At some point, saving money by keeping people off the pension while forgoing revenue to encourage them to make alternative provision becomes counter-productive. It could be simpler and fairer for the revenue forgone in superannuation concessions to be provided as a pension instead. Former professor Anthony Asher has called for the abolition of the age pension means test. This would cost $10 billion, he says, but $3 billion could be saved by taxing the resulting pensions, $1.8 billion by removing the senior tax offset, and $5.7 billion by removing the tax concessions for superannuation investment income.[28] He says that this would greatly simplify the system and remove distortions.

As well as being very expensive to government, superannuation tax breaks are too complex for most people to manage on their own. By adjusting the age at which it happened, there should be a fiscally neutral point at which the age pension means test could be abolished through ending future superannuation concessions. Ending super concessions would mean that there would be only one complex set of tax rules to deal with rather than two. Giving everyone over a certain age the pension (as was briefly the case for those over seventy-five under the Whitlam Government) could ultimately mean a simpler, and therefore a fairer, system.

It would be unfair, though, if changes to superannuation rules reduced the value or accessibility of people's existing entitlements. Despite being tax advantaged, super savings belong to individuals, not to society as a whole. Given that people invariably earn more working than on the pension and can access other forms of social security if they can't work, delaying access to the pension does not raise issues of fairness comparable to those potentially involved in changes to existing superannuation entitlements. Any changes to the superannuation regime would need to be 'grandfathered' so that people wouldn't lose existing access to what's already theirs.

The principal task of the next coalition government won't be directly stimulating the economy so much as trying to ensure that the economy is as productive as possible. It won't be directly creating jobs but nurturing the conditions under which jobs are most likely to be available. Of course, what happens today or tomorrow is important because, as Keynes quipped, 'in the long run, we're all dead'. Even so, effective government means not focusing on short-term fixes at the expense of good long-term policy. Australia's economic future depends on having more people—more people in the workforce and more people working more productively. In each area, the next coalition government will be able to build on the legacy of its predecessor and also, perhaps, to be more imaginative than the Howard Government felt it could be.

5 Australia's Biggest Political Problem and How to Fix It

For several days over Christmas in 2001, I was part of a crew at the Davidson rural fire station ready for deployment during a Sydney bushfire crisis. The prime minister had broken his holiday for a radio interview about the fires then ringing the city. The NSW government had deployed a giant 'Elvis' water-bombing helicopter, but more were needed and the premier was crying poor. Could the prime minister do something to save the city? Inevitably, he could. Since that time, the national government has half-funded at least three water bombers to help ensure that bushfire emergencies don't more often turn into tragedies. In this way, bushfire fighting, once solely the governmental responsibility of local councils but, by 2001, largely an instrumentality of the state government, became another of the many burdens that the national government had to shoulder.

More recently, the Rudd Government has formed a joint Commonwealth–state bushfire-recovery authority to help victims of the 2009 Victorian disaster. Unavoidably, this will give the Commonwealth serious political responsibility for rural fire services and land management, building codes and planning regimes in bush-fire-prone areas, even though it has no explicit constitutional authority whatsoever in these fields. Because the national government is involved, people will think that it is in charge or, at least, that it should be in charge. In fact, nothing will be possible without the consent of the Victorian government, and the history of cooperative ventures teaches that cooperation is only forthcoming while a crisis lasts and the Commonwealth is picking up the bill.

When the inescapable arguments begin over who should pay and how much, and the controversies rage over land management, one level of government will have the lion's share of political responsibility while another will have legal responsibility. The bushfire-recovery authority, which will almost certainly end up reporting to two masters but be answerable to neither, is likely to become another illustration of the way so much of Australia's governance has become a kind of constitutional three-legged race.

Not for a moment would the founding fathers have contemplated giving the Commonwealth responsibility for fire services. They could never have imagined the cost and sophistication of modern bushfire services, either. They did, though, fully accept that the constitution was a living document to be changed and reinterpreted as circumstances required. Of course, fire fighting could still be done by untrained volunteers putting tanks on utes and operating out of a local council shed. Still, it would be perverse to insist upon the perpetuation of that state of affairs when, in fact, the state governments' involvement in establishing state-wide rural fire services has dramatically improved them. Similarly, it would be perverse to insist that the Commonwealth stay out of fire fighting if the result of its involvement is the commitment of important extra resources and even further improvement in overall fire management. What matters is the establishment of the best possible services. Governmental structures should accommodate the country's needs, not vice versa.

Unfortunately, few areas of public discussion are as prone to political theology as relations between the Commonwealth and the states. On the one hand, there are those who regard the states as a mere accident of history to be abolished as soon as the necessary referendum would be likely to pass. On the other, there are those who mythologise the states as the ideal deliverers of complex services and as bulwarks against the allegedly dictatorial tendencies of the national government. In fact, the men who founded modern Australia weren't sentimental about the states. They knew that a federal structure was the only way to turn six colonies into one country. They also suspected that the continued existence of the states would mean less neglect of the regions by the national government. Still, if they had wanted to entrench for all time the arrangement of responsibilities applying at federation, they would not have provided for a High Court to interpret the constitution and a referendum mechanism to change it.

As long as particular levels of government continue to exist, it's important to give them meaningful tasks to perform. This doesn't mean that their existing tasks are the only ones that can ever legitimately be performed by that level of government. If it now makes sense for the national government to take on a particular role, that should happen. If it ever makes sense for a Commonwealth responsibility to be relinquished to the states, that should happen too, provided no one thinks that the Commonwealth won't be badgered to take it back as soon as there's a big public issue that a state is perceived to be mishandling.

It's almost an iron law of politics that voters will demand action from any level of government with a realistic prospect of making a difference. Ultimately, they will demand satisfaction from the highest level of government to which they have ready access. A premier can often plausibly say that a particular problem is too big for his government to handle. A prime minister, though, finds it much harder to handball responsibility to someone else. People sitting in seemingly endless traffic jams or waiting hours for distressed children to be seen in overcrowded hospitals aren't interested in technical distinctions about the particular roles of different levels of government. They just want their problems solved and become understandably angry with politicians who wring their hands and say that it's someone else's fault.

Inevitably, when nothing else seems to have made a difference, they expect the Commonwealth to 'do something'. This is why some mechanism needs to be established to give the Commonwealth legal authority to match its undoubted political and economic clout. Someone has to be in charge. Someone has to take responsibility. On the issues that matter, state premiers shouldn't be allowed to thumb their noses at the prime minister of the country lest the age-old judgment be pronounced against us that a house divided against itself cannot stand.

There are few problems in contemporary Australia that a dysfunctional federation doesn't make worse. The state governments have legal responsibility for issues that only the national government has the political authority and financial muscle to resolve. At present, the only effective way to improve public hospitals, for instance, or to better allocate Murray–Darling water or to establish a national school curriculum is for the Commonwealth to bribe the states. All too often the states take the money but fail to deliver the outcome. In large areas of our national life, no one is really in charge, because the Commonwealth funds the service but the state delivers it. Unlike a private contractor, a state government can't have its contract terminated. Hence, in these areas, the state governments tend to wield power without responsibility while the Commonwealth suffers responsibility without power.

More than fifty years of increasing Commonwealth involvement in areas of government that were once exclusively the realm of the states means that the federation is broken and does need to be fixed. The only credible way is to give the Commonwealth legal authority commensurate with its political responsibility. This is not 'centralising power in Canberra'. Rather, it's trying to ensure that political problems are subject to clear lines of responsibility and accountability. Prime Minister Rudd's pre-election talk about 'ending the blame game' was effective because voters want their problems solved. They don't want the states passing the buck to the Commonwealth and vice versa. Yet the blame game that voters so resent is unavoidable whenever two entities are trying to fix the same problem in different ways and neither one of them can effectively call the shots.

Responses to this dog's breakfast of divided responsibilities often involve proposals for a new federal compact with clearer distinctions about who does what and more revenue-raising powers given to the states. Unfortunately, no state took up the Fraser Government's offer of greater taxation powers and no one is seriously proposing that the national government should opt out of health or education. Another response is to propose the abolition of state governments, even though there is no reason the states can't continue to exercise the responsibilities that are still unquestionably theirs and there is little likelihood of voter support for such radical constitutional change.

For much of its time in office, the Howard Government wrestled in vain with the problem of recalcitrant states. Voters demanded better schools, hospitals, water management, and mental health and disability services, but the states rarely delivered, despite substantially increased Commonwealth funding. Much better performance would have required structural change that the states were not prepared to make. Although Howard-era Commonwealth–state funding agreements were more prescriptive than before and usually included performance targets, these were generally easy to fudge and were often not met because, the states said, their funding was still inadequate. There was rarely any penalty imposed for failure to meet performance targets, because docking the states' funding would just have made a bad situation worse.

One reason for the Howard Government's hesitation in tackling the dysfunctional federation was some conservatives' exaggerated respect for the states. It can't be stressed too much that Australia has states because it was the price of becoming a nation, not because the federation fathers thought that an intermediate level of government was necessary to avoid tyranny or that some services were inherently better delivered by states. When they praised federal systems they were making a virtue of necessity, not stating a philosophical principle. They certainly did not believe that a federal system was the only way to ensure effective government or to prevent autocracy. They were pragmatists determined to do what was necessary to produce a national government, not states' righters who thought that the compromises needed to bring about federation in 1901 should be preserved forever.

Indeed, much has changed over the last half century. Nearly always, it's been the Commonwealth taking an initiative of its own in an area that was hitherto a state responsibility or assisting the states to do their own job better. Since the 1940s, in response to problems or opportunities that the states had neglected, the Commonwealth has become successively involved in funding pharmaceutical drugs, universities, nursing homes, schools, medical services, hospitals, public housing, disability services and infrastructure. The Commonwealth is now expected to keep funding these services, even though it often has little or no say over how they're actually run. Constant bickering is the inevitable consequence, while voters become more and more fed up with demarcation disputes between different levels of government.

A Newspoll conducted for Griffith University, and published in July 2008[1], showed that 80.8 per cent of respondents thought that democracy works well in Australia but that only 67.8 per cent thought that the federal system works well. Further, 81.6 per cent rated the performance levels of the federal government as good, compared to only 56.9 per cent for state government. Tellingly, 50.1 per cent rated the federal government as the most effective level of government, compared to 19.9 per cent for local government and just 18.1 per cent for state government.

Most significantly, 79.2 per cent agreed that the statement closest to their view was: 'when there is an important issue that state governments are not solving, the federal government should step in to resolve it'. Although 51.8 per cent agreed that 'it is better for decisions to be made at the lowest level of government competent to deal with the decision', the contradiction between these positions may be more apparent than real. When it comes to practical problem solving rather than abstract principles, people seem to want the national government to lead. Only 17.4 per cent agreed with the statement that 'the federal government should not get involved in issues that are the responsibility of state governments'. On these figures, Australians support the federal system but overwhelmingly want it to work better. They don't want to abolish the states but don't like argument over who's really in charge and think, when push comes to shove, that final authority should rest with the national government.

It's not surprising that contemporary Australians should rate the national government much more highly than the other governments. We've now had more than 100 years to watch our constitution and system of government in action. There have been some very good state governments (the Kennett and Greiner Governments are recent examples), but mostly they seem better at requesting Commonwealth help (and then running interference on its delivery) than at actually running their own states.

In 1901, the states were the highest level of government to which Australians had reasonably direct access. Odd though it now seems, Australia was then more of a geographical entity than a focus of loyalty. That came gradually over the ensuing century. In those days, Australia was at least as much an assemblage of states as it was a nation. When they weren't to the mother country and its empire, people's sentimental attachments were largely to the states. A hundred years on, the states retain their constitutional standing but have almost totally lost their place in people's loyalties. People in Perth or Hobart may still feel politically vulnerable and prone to official neglect but, even in the outlying regions, they have less sense than ever of state patriotism.

A century ago, Sir Robert Garran described federalism as 'a form of government in which sovereign or political power is divided between the central and the local governments so that each of them within its own sphere is independent of the other'. It's a long time since Australia has been a true federal system under this definition. In Australia, state governments have not been independent of the Commonwealth government, even in their 'own sphere', at least since the uniform tax case of 1942 established the Commonwealth's fiscal supremacy. In many of their areas of responsibility, the states have long expected Commonwealth help. As well, in most areas of life, Australians increasingly expect national leadership. This is the practical reality that constitutional purists tend to ignore.

There has been a lot of myth making about federal systems, much of it an echo of the American pre–Civil War argument for states' rights. Greg Craven, now vice-chancellor of the Australian Catholic University, has eulogised federalism as 'designed to protect those qualities of freedom, balance, community and difference dear to liberals and conservatives'.[2] That was not, in fact, what the federation fathers had in mind. As well, it would have been news to the English statesmen who first realised these ideals through the Westminster parliament and who certainly didn't think that they needed devolution or a federation to bring them about.

The commitment to the states of some Australian conservatives contrasts with British conservatives' preference for a strong central government. In 1998 the British Conservative leader William Hague said that it was a unitary rather than a federal arrangement that ensured there was no conflict of power or confusion of accountability. Britain, he said, was blessedly 'free of the kind of paralysing disputes between national parliaments and regional parliaments or between state governments and federal governments that are so common in other political systems'.[3] Showing a shrewd understanding of the way federal systems can operate in practice, he predicted that the establishment of a Scottish parliament would mean that 'Edinburgh will blame every poorly run hospital or failing school on lack of resources from Westminster. Westminster will blame Edinburgh for spending resources badly. And the people will not know who to blame'.[4] To UK conservatives, what mattered was not a multiplicity of power sources but clear lines of democratic accountability.

Australian conservatives' attachments might be understandable if the states had cultural identities as distinctive as those of Wales or Scotland, but they plainly don't. No British conservative supported the creation of new assemblies in Scotland and Wales on the grounds of 'subsidiarity'. In the United Kingdom, the notion that services should be delivered by the smallest unit capable of delivering them didn't mean the creation of an intermediate level of government. Instead, it meant strong local governments effectively delivering local services.

According to Craven, 'federalism ensures that the policy issues closest to regional communities are determined substantially by those communities' by committing those issues 'to local state governments rather than the remote bureaucracy of Canberra'.[5] Apart from idealising state-government bureaucrats, this is more an argument for strong local government than for the states. As John Howard once said, 'there is often less to these arguments than meets the eye ... The view that state governments have benign decentralist tendencies has always been something of a myth'.[6] As Howard knew, the theory of federalism is fine. It's the practice that is the problem. Politicians who want to be elected, though, can't justify what doesn't work in practice by saying that it should work in theory.

Undoubtedly, the most far-fetched argument for the states is that they form a supposed bulwark against the potential tyranny of the national government—as if Australians' freedoms are more fragile than those of Britons or New Zealanders and need the states for their protection. Unfortunately for federalist theory, it's very hard to find any recent example of bad Commonwealth policy that the states have stopped or an example of good policy in one state that the others have then been forced to adopt (at least since Queensland's abolition of death duties in the 1970s).

In contemporary Australia, there is a yawning gulf between classic federalism and governmental practice and voter expectations. Health, education and the environment are the clear constitutional responsibility of the states but are also the areas of government policy that voters typically nominate as most important. This is why even the most federally minded leaders, such as Sir Robert Menzies with universities, for instance, and Malcolm Fraser with the environment, have ended up increasing the relative size and importance of the national government.

On gun laws, workplace-relations change, the development of an academically rigorous national school curriculum, and protecting the Murray–Darling basin, to name only the most obvious instances of policy tension with the states, John Howard was more interested in solving problems than in constitutional niceties. To put it another way, he was more interested in realising his conception of liberal-conservative political values than in preserving a constitutional orthodoxy that had passed its 'use-by' date.

As members of the Howard cabinet knew only too well, working with the states was rarely straightforward. Often, state support for Commonwealth objectives or even agreement on specific policy detail did not guarantee an outcome. In mid-2004, to give an every-day example, Canberra committed $6 million towards the establishment of a much-needed radiation oncology centre at Lismore on the NSW north coast. This would have meant less invasive treatment and significantly higher survival rates for local people with cancer. The state government welcomed this initiative but said that it couldn't start building the centre till mid-2007. Early in 2007, without any real explanation, but presumably because it had other priorities, the state government unilaterally delayed the start till 2010 at the earliest.

From 2005, the Howard Government sought to begin rolling out a national bowel cancer screening program. This was a 2004 election commitment, based on a successful pilot scheme that showed that screening could prevent dozens of people a year from contracting bowel cancer. For screening to happen, though, state governments needed to supply registry data so that test kits could be mailed to people turning fifty-five or sixty-five. Because of the procrastination of some states, this relatively simple program took almost an entire term of government to become fully operational. The states used it as an opportunity to demand more funding for public hospital colonoscopies, even though screening would ultimately save hospitals from treating more people with advanced cancer.

In June 2007, the Howard Government announced its intention to take over and directly fund the Mersey hospital, which the Tasmanian government planned to downgrade. The Commonwealth's move was a response to local pressure but also provided an opportunity to showcase running a hospital through a local board rather than a state department. Although the Tasmanian government reluctantly agreed to the takeover (the federal opposition also supported it but reversed this position once in government), it tried to sabotage the operation of the hospital by instructing doctors based elsewhere to withdraw clinical support.

These frustrations with the states were not unique to the Howard Government. For instance, Victoria has only just signed up to the former government's $10 billion Murray–Darling plan, after the Rudd Government committed a further $1 billion to water initiatives. Despite this, South Australia has threatened an eleventh-hour High Court challenge. Prior to the 2007 election, the then opposition promised an education revolution based on providing every secondary-school student with access to a computer. A leaked letter revealed the Rudd Government's intention to offer the NSW government additional funding for an unrelated project in order to compensate for the state's extra costs in servicing computers and training students in their use. When the exposed side deal was not forthcoming, New South Wales initially refused to take the computers, leaving its students potentially disadvantaged. In the end, the Rudd Government had to bribe the states by almost doubling their program funding.

As long as the economic boom lasted, Australians' instinctive sense of grievance against government largely focused on the inadequacies of services delivered by the states. One of the paradoxes of the 2007 election was the perverse way federal Labor benefited from state Labor governments' failures. When voters complained about poor public hospitals, public schools and public transport, John Howard correctly observed that these were state responsibilities. By contrast, Kevin Rudd capitalised on voter anger by promising to work with the states to solve the problems that state-government ineptitude had largely brought about.

As Rudd is now discovering, the new prime minister can no more force the states to address the entrenched problems in state service delivery than his predecessor could. Emboldened public-sector unions are probably even less likely to agree to reform under the current government than they were under the previous one. The premiers are more polite to Rudd than they were to Howard in his final year but no more inclined to take hard decisions at his request. Why would they? At present, they are masters in their own house but can half-plausibly blame someone else when things go wrong.

The problem with the Rudd version of 'cooperative federalism' is that it has no mechanism for resolving disagreements except goodwill and money, neither of which is in limitless supply. Unless it is clearly in their interests to do so (and sometimes not even then), the states are generally averse to cooperating with the national government. They will pay lip-service to national goals and gladly accept large amounts of Commonwealth funding in order to achieve them while continuing to pursue their own political objectives.

The routine is nearly always the same. Commonwealth–state summits generate headlines about agreements in principle, which rarely materialise because the states demand too high a price, don't really want their officials to agree on the detail or don't treat harmonisation legislation as a high parliamentary priority. In this way, the pursuit of national reforms becomes a frustrating political merry-go-round, always needing just one more meeting or just another funding agreement to finalise.

To take a particularly vexing example, there are still numerous professional and trade qualifications that are not recognised in other states, even though Bob Hawke and Nick Greiner first announced mutual recognition at a premiers' conference nearly twenty years ago. Typically, a recent evaluation report noted 'considerable support' for moves to what was described as national licensing but 'no commonality or agreement on the exact form such national licensing should take'.[7]

The Commonwealth and the states first agreed to support a national school curriculum in 1986 and established a national curriculum corporation in 1990. Despite repeated agreements in principle and statements of intent, a 2007 report found that only physics and chemistry had 'a high degree of national curriculum consistency'. If the recently appointed National Curriculum Board, with a $20 million budget, can meet the latest timeline for a national curriculum by 2011, this relatively straightforward project will have taken a mere quarter century to complete.

Under the current Australian Health Care Agreements, in return for Commonwealth funding, state public hospitals are supposed to see patients within clinically acceptable time frames depending on their condition. This does not happen in about 20 per cent of cases. The states claim that their failure is due to the Commonwealth's inadequate funding. For its part, all Canberra can do to force the states to perform is withhold a portion of their funds, even though it's plainly self-defeating to seek to solve a problem by aggravating its cause.

The only effective way to tackle public-hospital problems is to change the way they are managed. This would require the states, among other things, to challenge the health-sector unions. Because this is a risk that state governments have been unwilling to take, hospital reform is stymied as long as the Commonwealth government has no power to direct the states. The people with the potential will to change lack the authority. The people with the authority to change lack the will. Given the extra money that it will almost certainly involve, hospital reform is probably a job that's beyond state governments, especially since divided responsibilities provide a convenient excuse for inaction.

Prime Minister Rudd seemed to recognise this when he said, pre-election, that he would work with the states for eighteen months and then proceed to take over public hospitals if their performance did not improve. The commitment generated much supportive comment even though it is highly unlikely ever to be carried out and now seems to have been abandoned. No state would agree to a takeover of its hospitals other than on terms that no Commonwealth government would accept (such as, for instance, surrendering private schools to the states). Seeking to change the constitution to give the Commonwealth specific authority over public hospitals would be an implicit vote of no-confidence in state Labor governments that no Labor prime minister could plausibly undertake.

'Cooperative federalism' and 'ending the blame game' were effective rhetorical devices to defuse the political problem of potential wall-to-wall Labor governments. The formulation of slogans, though, doesn't change the actual business of government. As matters stand, endless turf wars, agreements that turn out to mean much less than they seem, and glacial progress towards obvious goals are the best that can be expected in areas that require Commonwealth funding for state government services or state government cooperation for the establishment of national rules or standards.

By contrast, a striking example of what can be achieved when one level of government is clearly in charge was the Howard Government's intervention into remote NT townships. This was not only a potential watershed in Aboriginal policy but a good illustration of what the national government can do when it's not subject to state-government veto. In this case, the Commonwealth was able to mobilise NT government personnel and co-opt NT institutions because the Territory is a subordinate legislature subject ultimately to the Commonwealth parliament. The *Little Children Are Sacred* report was certainly not the first credible report detailing horrific violence in Aboriginal families. It was, though, the first report that dealt just with a territory. It was the first report confined to places where Canberra could, if necessary, 'pull rank' and call the shots.

Although some prominent people, including the then NT deputy chief minister and the local federal MP, described the intervention as 'racist' and an 'invasion', most Australians thought that it was self-evidently necessary to deal with such serious and entrenched problems. Indeed, with 20/20 hindsight, many thought that the intervention measures should have been taken years earlier and extended to all remote Aboriginal settlements, not just those in the Territory. This 'more, please' reaction ignored the fact that territory governments are subject to the Commonwealth in a way that state governments are not. At the time of the intervention, Indigenous affairs minister Mal Brough had offered to fund and organise similar measures in the remote townships of the Kimberley—which had Australia's highest reported rates of sexual infection among minors—but was brushed off by the WA government.

The intervention was a dramatic illustration of the Commonwealth's capacity to make change for the better where it's the sovereign level of government. What could be done in the Territory contrasts with what couldn't be done in the states. Where a state government sits on its hands in an area of its constitutional responsibility (as the NT government had hitherto done with the *Little Children Are Sacred* report), the national government can try to buy a solution, but it can't actually make one happen.

Calls for a more constructive relationship between the different levels of government or for leaders to put the country above their sectional or political interests ignore the constitutional facts and take for granted a level of magnanimity that politicians don't normally have. A genuine crisis or rare gifts of character on the part of leaders might temporarily cause antagonists to make common cause. Mostly, though, exhortations to work together boost the self-regard of the people making them (and possibly touch the consciences of decision-makers) but make very little difference to the way governments operate.

If, as Australians seem to want, the national government is to resolve problems that the states can't handle, there will have to be constitutional change. The simplest way to do this would be a constitutional amendment to provide that the Commonwealth parliament can make laws generally for the peace, order and good government of the country. Putting a full stop after 'Commonwealth' in the first sentence of section 51 of the Constitution would mean that the national government could propose laws in all areas, not just those currently listed. It wouldn't abolish the states but, because Commonwealth law prevails over state law to the extent of any inconsistency, it would mean that they could not jeopardise policy in areas where the national government was determined to intervene.

If this was perceived as too much of a 'power grab', reform could require, say, two votes of the parliament separated by six months for a particular Commonwealth law, not otherwise constitutionally authorised, to prevail over state law.

The appendix to this book contains a draft bill for a referendum to bring about such a change. This would be akin to the disallowance provisions that currently apply to territory laws. Even under such an arrangement, though, the national government would be unlikely to seek unilaterally to resolve issues about water licences, hospital funding, information sharing and so on. To intervene too readily would almost certainly strike voters as bullying and be punished at the ballot box. The states would continue to administer these matters. The Commonwealth would only seek to force their hand if it felt that the national interest demanded it.

As with the territories, it's likely that such a power would not often be used, because the states would less often be contrary. Whether this resulted in the 'withering away of the states' (as I once proposed) would depend on their performance. State governments that let the Commonwealth set national standards while delivering efficient services would be at very little risk of interference. On the other hand, overriding state governments that were bloody-minded or incompetent (without actually replacing them) would be less undemocratic than state governments appointing administrators to run dysfunctional councils.

It's conventional wisdom that referendums fail without bipartisan support. During the time of the Fraser Government, just a few maverick senators helped to defeat a proposal preventing separate elections for the House and the Senate. Putting a proposal to a referendum certainly has no guarantee of success. On the other hand, not putting a proposal absolutely guarantees failure. It leaves governments with the same options that have led us to the current impasse.

It's democracy rather than politicians' hubris that exposes the national government to inexorable mission creep. Because there is no realistic prospect of the Commonwealth returning significant responsibilities to the states nor of the states agreeing to take on additional revenue-raising possibilities, the only way to sort out responsibilities in areas where the two levels of government are both involved is to put one level of government in overall charge. The only practical alternatives are to accept the existing situation as the least-worst outcome or to give the national government power it does not currently have to bring the states into line. Of course, no sensible national government would want to interfere if the states were running hospitals, schools and transport systems effectively. If they're not, though, and the problem is going from bad to worse with ramifications for the country at large, why should the national government remain no more than a well-meaning bystander? A government that wanted to be re-elected would only exercise its newfound authority in extremis or to try to prevent bloody-mindedness from sabotaging sensible coordination between the states.

The status quo would be more acceptable if the likes of Kennett and Greiner were still running state governments. Instead, the states are seen as the second XI of Australian politics. As participants know, there is little prospect of Commonwealth–state summits departing from the current headmaster-meets-student-representatives-on-an-equal-footing format. The problem with the Council of Australian Governments (COAG) is that its processes have no authority of their own and its decisions are not binding.

European institutions have more authority over Britain and France than COAG has over New South Wales and Victoria. The ANU's Professor John Wanna has suggested that meetings of Commonwealth and state chief ministers and ministers should operate like a cabinet.[8] This would require the states to accept Commonwealth leadership—which is precisely what they won't do under the current constitutional arrangements—or, equally unlikely, the Commonwealth government to accept that it could be outvoted by the states (which used to be the case with the Loan Council when the states had more clout).

Of course, the extra authority that would have enabled the Howard Government, say, to implement a national curriculum stressing narrative history would also have enabled the Keating Government, say, to override Liberal WA workplace laws. Unavoidably, under such circumstances, Commonwealth governments would have more scope to implement their policy and to realise their values regardless of whether their values were conservative and liberal or radical and socialist.

Preserving the states in their current role theoretically makes it harder for misguided national governments to implement poor policy. In his article 'Ten Advantages of a Federal Constitution', Professor Geoffrey Walker talks about Canberra's 'attacks on civil and political rights'.[9] Whether the two specific examples he gives, the Fraser Government's retrospective tax legislation and the Hawke Government's Australia Card bill, really fall into such a category is debatable. In any event, the states had nothing to do with thwarting either policy. Nor were the states any use in thwarting other policies (such as border protection) that some (wrongly, in my view) found unconscionable.

By contrast, the states are much more often a brake on good government than on bad. It's much easier to find examples of sensible national reforms being frustrated by the states than a case of the Commonwealth blocking the states' innovations. Perhaps the Howard Government's opposition to selling the Snowy Mountains authority could be seen as a recent example of the Commonwealth running interference on the states. In this case, though, the Commonwealth had been taking the political heat for a sale that would overwhelmingly have benefited the states. As majority shareholders, New South Wales and Victoria could have overcome the Commonwealth veto had they really wanted to.

The no-change position boils down to the contention that the national government is more likely to get it wrong than right, so the less it can do the better. It's essentially an argument for weak government. Craven admitted as much when he boasted that federalism ensures 'that no single government in Australia can do anything, anywhere, any time'.[10] In fact, the ballot box is a much better defence against bad policy than interference from another level of government.

Only in federalist theory are the states potential laboratories for innovative new policy. In practice, conformist mediocrity is much more common than creative experimentation in state service delivery. The introduction of case-mix public-hospital funding in Victoria is sometimes cited as an illustration of pioneering work in an individual state, but Victoria actually needed Commonwealth government help to adopt it. In any event, the other states' failure to adopt case-mix suggests that a good example is not as powerful or persuasive as arm-twisting by Canberra.

Giving more authority to the national government is not the same as supporting big government over small. Unlike the states, which typically provide services through giant government-run organisations (exemplified by public schools, public hospitals and public transport), the Commonwealth usually provides services through non-government bodies. With the de-monopolisation and privatisation of Telstra, Australia Post is the only significant consumer service still delivered through a Commonwealth monolith. Commonwealth-funded medical, pharmaceutical, aged care, educational and employment services are nearly all provided through non-government entities. Greater

Commonwealth provision of, say, disability services is almost certain to mean funding people to purchase services rather than creating a new federal bureaucracy.

As John Howard said in 2005, accusations of centralism misunderstood the then government's purpose in changing the 'federal-state balance'. It was to 'expand individual choice, freedom and opportunity'. The goal, he said, was 'to free the individual' rather than 'to trample on the states'.[11] Far from producing a bigger, stronger public sector, what might be described as 'conservative centralism' is likely to reduce the total size of government. Perhaps through history and inertia more than instinct, even Labor governments in Canberra have often turned out to be less 'socialist' than coalition governments in the states.

If the services for which the national government is responsible are delivered by a range of private, religious, charitable and community-based providers, while the services for which the state governments are responsible are delivered by centrally run bureaucracies, the conservative instinct should be to support more Commonwealth services and fewer state ones. To the extent that they argue for continued state control of public hospitals, schools and transport systems, at least in an Australian context, conservatives are supporting socialist service-delivery systems over market-based ones.

On this score, the logic of the states' rights position is that theory trumps practice. It's better to let a supposedly close-to-the-people government run services badly than to allow a supposedly remote-from-the-people government to run services well, often by contracting their management to local people. Apart from the inherent implausibility of the proposition that, say, New South Wales's forty-nine members of the House of Representatives are somehow less close to the people who elect them than their ninety-nine state parliamentary counterparts, conservative states' righters are in the odd position of defending mediocre-at-delivering-services bureaucracies. It's hardly an affront to the conservative instinct to give more authority to the least interfering level of government, especially if this means utilising the mechanisms to change the constitution that the federal fathers so wisely gave us.

If the national government were to become responsible for public schools or public hospitals, for instance, Canberra would be most likely to provide funding, set policy parameters and maintain quality rather than to directly deliver services. For some time, the state governments would probably continue to provide existing services but with different and stronger accountability mechanisms. Eventually, free public hospital and public school services would most likely be provided on a contestable basis by a range of independent and autonomous organisations as well as by state-government instrumentalities. The Commonwealth government would not run the service but ensure that a professional service was being provided.

Former NSW Labor treasurer Michael Costa had some good advice for Kevin Rudd prior to last November's COAG meeting:

> He should end the health blame game by announcing that the federal Government has responsibility for all aspects of national health care, including funding and administration of the public hospital system. He should phase in a new administrative and financial structure for health over a five- to seven-year period. The first phase should begin with the present healthcare agreements, with all additional federal funds being contingent on the states agreeing to the new framework. The states, in conjunction with the federal Government, should begin the introduction of a system of standardised information collation based on episode funding within a properly constructed and administered purchaser provider model. Greater autonomy and accountability needs to be established at the local level.
>
> During the second phase, hospital-level competition on quality and cost effectiveness of service provision should be introduced.[12]

It's significant that a former state treasurer thought that sensible reforms of this nature could only come about through Commonwealth government pressure. None of this, as it happened, had been attempted by the state government of which Costa had been a significant part. In fact, all that the Rudd Government actually secured at COAG in return for an additional $15 billion in Commonwealth health funding was more information. As well, the prime minister's former commitment to constitutional change, should the states not lift their game, was quietly dropped from the ALP website. A week later, Costa commented that Rudd had 'failed to achieve fundamental structural reform ... Like the faint-hearted lion in the Wizard of Oz', he lacked 'the political courage to end the blame game'.[13] In fairness to Rudd, though, it should be said that this would have been much easier if the Commonwealth had a constitutional mechanism to resolve an argument.

Instinctive politician that he was, John Howard understood that the states were no longer a locus of loyalty. Nationalism and localism, he thought, the country and the neighbourhood engaged people, not the states. 'Rivers do not recognise lines on the map that we call state borders', he once said. 'The core problem is that the states have competing interests ... We must think and act as Australians, not Queenslanders, Victorians or New South Welshmen'.[14] 'If we were starting again', he said, 'I wouldn't support the existing state structures ... I would actually support having a national government and perhaps a series of regional governments having the powers, say, of the Brisbane City Council'.[15] Of course, we can't start again, as every conservative knows, including the former prime minister. For conservatives, the issue is whether any change is clearly worth the risks and costs. Giving the national government a further option of the type it can already exercise over the states in some instances and can exercise over the territories in all instances should minimise the risk of change.

The former prime minister's 'ideal position' was that both levels of government should fully meet their responsibilities. 'Our first impulse', he said, would be 'to seek cooperation with states and territories on national challenges where there is overlapping responsibility'.[16] But what happens when the states refuse to cooperate or expect to be bribed at an unacceptably high price? Plainly, across a whole range of important national challenges such as water, education, infrastructure and health, cooperation was not readily forthcoming once summitry's warm innerglow had faded.

Tackling the dysfunctional federation turned out to be a lost opportunity for the Howard Government. Traditionalists who might otherwise have rejected change could have been reassured by John Howard's undoubted conservatism. Certainly, it would have been a political objective worthy of a great prime minister. It could have been the principal element in the fifth-term agenda that people ultimately concluded the government lacked. Perhaps the former prime minister eventually judged that it needed more political capital than an 11-year-old government could muster.

By contrast, voters are unlikely to trust a 'control freak' (as Kevin Rudd is reputed to be) with reform of Commonwealth–state relations. Besides, too many of the state governments will still be in Labor hands, at least for the remainder of this Commonwealth parliamentary term. Accepting the primacy of the national government, even in principle, would be a 'big ask' of serving premiers. Even the strongest national Labor government would find the state Labor machines very hard to cross, let alone a prime minister who is better at talking about problems than proposing change.

Fixing the federation is almost certain to be a challenge for the next coalition government. Change that is contemporary, practical and incremental is just the kind of policy that a revitalised Liberal Party should adopt. As long as eight out of ten Australians think that the Commonwealth should be able to resolve problems that the states can't handle, a proposal to give the national government the authority to do so is the kind of pragmatism they should like.

6 Making the States Do Better

In every survey, health and education top the list of voters' concerns. Newspoll results show that only once in the past decade has any other issue briefly eclipsed them. That was water security in February 2007. To voters, health and education outrank unemployment, the environment, national security, tax, workplace relations and immigration (important though these undoubtedly are). Voters seem to consider health and education more important, even, than economic management, notwithstanding the fact that good economic management is a precondition, in the long run, for better hospitals and schools.

It's precisely because voters take health and education so seriously that the Commonwealth government has become increasingly involved in these areas, directly funding visits to the doctor, for instance, and funding the states' schools and hospitals in ways that our constitutional founders could scarcely have imagined. Because voters think that health and education are so important, it's hard to imagine the revival of a political party that basically says that 'these are subjects for the states' or even that policies in this area depend on working with the states.

Whenever enough voters think that state governments are neglecting an important issue, the Commonwealth ends up becoming involved. The Commonwealth first became involved in funding pharmaceuticals because, in the 1940s, the states refused widely to subsidise access to 'wonder drugs' such as penicillin. In the 1960s, the Commonwealth started to subsidise nursing homes because the states were felt to be making inadequate provision. At about the same time, Commonwealth schools funding began because the states were failing to fund science blocks. University funding commenced because of a widespread perception that fees penalised students from badly off families; again, the states would not address the issue.

Commonwealth spending on health and education now approaches $90 billion a year, or about a quarter of its total spending. It's all in areas that were once wholly the preserve of the states. Most of it is not directly authorised by the constitution other than via specific-purpose grants under section 96. Still, any withdrawal of Commonwealth involvement or spending in these areas would rightly be seen as a cop out.

Because the Commonwealth lacks specific authority in these areas, it usually ends up funding services that other entities actually deliver. In the case of funding for pharmaceutical, medical and aged care services and in the case of private hospital, private school and university spending, the Commonwealth essentially funds individual choice. But with public school and public hospital services, the Commonwealth supports services that are directed and delivered by the state governments. It's one thing for the Commonwealth to fund citizens' choices, another to fund the choices of state governments, yet that's hard to avoid as long as the national government has no constitutional authority over the states' health and education systems.

Most Australians instinctively support health and education reform because they sense that the existing highly bureaucratic structures are unresponsive to people's needs. Meaningful reform, though, is unlikely until one level of government can call the shots. As long as reform involves negotiations with the states, reform proposals will nearly always mean that the Commonwealth pays for changes that the states then have to deliver—a recipe for buck passing and blame shifting—or that an unwieldy state bureaucracy is replaced by an equally unwieldy and possibly even less accountable joint

Commonwealth–state bureaucracy. Without specific constitutional authority over health and education or without general authority over the states, Commonwealth-sponsored schemes of reform are largely fated to fail because the states control the structures that deliver the services.

The states will gladly take the Commonwealth's money, but are most unlikely ever to change their bureaucratic structures as long as problems can plausibly be attributed to the Commonwealth's parsimony rather than to their own addiction to bureaucracy. As Michael Costa has observed, the NSW government in particular has used the proceeds of the long boom to boost public sector numbers and pay.[1] After all, more public employees mean comparatively stronger unions, a larger 'client class' dependent on government, and, superficially at least, the appearance of better services for the public.

Without extra authority over the states (of the type I argue for in the previous chapter), there's an element of wishful thinking in much Commonwealth policy on education and health. The Rudd Government, for instance, has promised to provide 'universal' preschool education. As things stand, no Commonwealth government can deliver a commitment of this type. It could impose further requirements on Commonwealth-funded childcare centres. It could provide additional funding to the states for preschools. Only state governments, though, can compel parents to send their kids to school at a certain age. Without ultimate authority over the states, Commonwealth ministers can strike a pose over public schools and hospitals, but they can't guarantee to deliver a policy. Still, the Commonwealth's influence is considerable and it's worth considering how it should be exerted.

Better Hospitals

Historically, the states and territories were responsible for all health services that weren't provided by private arrangement between patients and health professionals. The states provided subsidised or (in Queensland) free hospital treatment for people electing to be public patients. As well, they provided free or subsidised community health services to the chronically ill. People who were without private insurance, though, or who didn't request special treatment often faced significant bills. Because of concerns about two classes of patients, those who could afford to pay and those who couldn't and were too proud to request fee relief, the Commonwealth introduced Medibank in 1975 and then Medicare in 1984, a universal Commonwealth government–funded insurance scheme to meet most of the costs of medical treatment.

Since then, the Commonwealth has become increasingly responsible for all health services not provided to public patients in public hospitals. Even the public hospital systems have come to be about half funded by the Commonwealth, in return for the states continuing to provide free treatment to public patients in public hospitals. The Commonwealth has also increasingly funded the states' population health services such as immunisation.

There is a range of perennial issues with health services, including those that the Commonwealth government funds. Mostly, these revolve around waiting times for non-emergency treatment in public hospitals and the cost to patients of health services that aren't provided there. They reflect the unavoidable fact that sought-after services will be rationed by price or by waiting list. Then there are 'human error' issues that can't always be avoided in circumstances where fallible human beings, however professional and carefully supervised, are dealing with life-and-death problems under great pressure.

Scandals such as the so-called Dr Death case in Queensland show how normally effective regulatory systems, under community and official pressure to sanction a wider range of services, can ignore problems long after they should have been identified and dealt with. Scandals such as that involving the maternity unit at Camden Hospital in New South Wales in 2005 show how political pressure can produce inadequately staffed and funded institutions that can't consistently deliver a professional service.

When it comes to free services, there can easily be a mismatch between what governments promise and what they are prepared to pay for. Under these circumstances, the professional health staff—the doctors and nurses who actually have to deal with patients—are often required to do more with less. Sooner or later, individuals and institutions react to the strain. Individuals resign and institutions become dysfunctional. To a greater or lesser extent, this is the problem that bedevils public hospital systems right around Australia.

In comparison to the highly publicised disasters and ongoing crises in state public hospitals, it's fair to say that the problems that have arisen in the Commonwealth-run parts of the health system have usually been well managed. There were occasional public complaints over the speed of approval processes for new drugs (such as the cancer drug Herceptin) or the methodology for funding new technology (such as PET scanning). The sharp fall in GP bulk-billing between the late '90s and 2003 had an impact on public confidence in Commonwealth health programs. Even so, the issue was not the quality of the service but its affordability. The government introduced new incentive payments, which fairly quickly restored bulk-billing to record levels. The medical-indemnity crisis of 2003, when hundreds of private specialists threatened to withdraw services from public hospitals, was not of the Commonwealth's making, but the Howard Government had to resolve it. It quickly hammered out support arrangements for medical-indemnity insurance, which again made premiums affordable.

In addition, the Howard Government made health services generally more affordable through extensions of Medicare to cover allied-health professional treatment for chronic disease and mental health, the improved Medicare safety net to help people whose out-of-pocket, out-of-hospital expenses exceeded a certain threshold, and subsidies for private health insurance for private hospital treatment and for allied-health professional consultations.

By contrast, the states have invariably responded bureaucratically to problems in professional service delivery in public hospitals. Typically, a problem in maternity services, for instance, wouldn't be addressed primarily through employing more obstetricians and midwives but through tighter controls and greater accountability measures. A classic illustration of the states' addiction to bureaucracy was the NSW government's response to the recommendations of the Garling report. Instead of employing more nurses and reducing the paperwork expected of them, the state government promised to appoint 500 extra clerical assistants so that the paperwork could be better handled. The end result is that very many public hospital doctors and nurses feel that they are the 'meat in the sandwich' between budget-obsessed administrators and patients unhappy about unreasonable waits for important treatment.

The Garling report, published late in 2008, captures much of the frustration and despair of professional health staff who think that their dedication and skill is being taken for granted and exploited. Although the report deals with New South Wales, the problems it described and analysed reflect those to be found in public hospitals throughout the country. Lack of funding and shortages of professional staff are certainly issues, but an even more basic problem is a governance structure that deprives professionals and administrators on the spot of any real freedom of action. Trivial decisions have to be referred 'higher up'. As one very senior doctor, a leading clinician in his field, once told me, he didn't have the authority to order a plate of sandwiches for a meeting despite his role as clinical director of 1500 professional staff on a combined payroll of about $100 million a year. The only actual executive authority that his position conferred was that of chairing meetings.

Perhaps hamstrung by his terms of reference, Garling's recommendations were much less stark than his findings. Garling did not support the re-introduction of local hospital boards, even though many of those who gave evidence thought that this would be the best way to empower local health professionals and managers. In New South Wales, local hospital boards had been whittled away and ultimately abolished by the 1990s because, it was thought, they were an obstacle to rationalising services. There's no doubt that a local hospital board can be a significant obstacle to head office—but this is precisely the point. When head office is intent on cost savings, patients and the people treating them need champions. Head office should have to win the argument rather than just give an order. Under the current arrangements, public hospital doctors and nurses find themselves at the wrong end of a long chain of command.

In the run-up to the 2007 election, the Howard Government announced, as a condition of access to new Commonwealth funding for local hospital infrastructure projects, that hospitals with more than fifty beds should have their own board. The board would appoint the local CEO and, together with the CEO, manage the hospital's budget. Another condition was that the hospital would itself keep any private income or donations without a commensurate reduction in state government funding. Of course, hospitals would still have been required to deliver services in accordance with the standards set by the relevant professional body. The state governments would still have given each hospital its funding and broadly determined the services that each hospital would deliver. It would have meant, though, that decisions about equipment purchases, staffing levels, and pay over and above any relevant general determination would be made at the local level. If a department needed more staff, a decision could be made on the spot. If a doctor wanted to reduce a waiting list, suitable arrangements could be juggled by officials at the hospital.

Local boards wouldn't resolve the inevitable tension between finite resources and almost infinite demand for services or the myriad stresses generated by internal hospital politics, but they would at least mean that decisions would be made by people in daily contact with the patients and staff affected by them. Without a substantial measure of local autonomy and the consequent sense of local 'ownership', public hospitals are unlikely to regain the team spirit that they need to function at their best. Because there will be no serious revival of morale among public hospital staff without these changes, they should continue to be Liberal Party policy.

The Howard Government had planned to use the 2008 Health Care Agreement negotiations to try to ensure that the states ran public hospitals the way the former government would have done if it had possessed the authority to do so. The experience of previous negotiations in 1998 and 2003, and the gulf between what the states had then promised and what they had delivered, meant that the Howard Government would not again have accepted the states' assurances about meeting key performance indicators. These were part of the

2003 agreements but, in many instances, had either been fudged or just not been met. Instead, in its naivety, the new government essentially reproduced the former agreements with the same talk of fresh starts and working together, but with the same near certainty of failure to achieve lasting improvements, because the same unwieldy and unresponsive bureaucracies were still in place.

Because it funds specific services or individual patients, the Commonwealth's approach to health is fundamentally different from that of the states, which provide services themselves through large public-sector organisations. Through Medicare, the Commonwealth funds patients to buy medical services or directly funds bulk-billing doctors. Through the Pharmaceutical Benefits Scheme (PBS), the Commonwealth funds pharmacists and companies to provide subsidised drugs. Through aged-care funding, the Commonwealth supports independent institutions to deliver services that individuals or their families choose to use. By contrast, except for a mere handful of privately owned public hospitals (such as St Vincent's in Sydney and Melbourne), state health departments directly provide public hospital services.

The difference between the indirectly provided services and the directly provided ones is that, in the former cases, patient choice rather than official decision drives resource allocation. John Howard was right to express scepticism about whether Commonwealth bureaucrats would be better at running hospitals than their state counterparts, but wrong to imply that a Commonwealth assumption of responsibility for public hospitals would just swap one lot of bureaucrats for another. What matters is not so much which level of government is responsible for public hospitals but how that level of government chooses to run them. The argument for making public hospitals a Commonwealth responsibility is not based on the inherently greater wisdom of Commonwealth public servants but on the Commonwealth's confirmed predisposition to run health services in a very different way.

In the 1980s the Liberal Party opposed Medicare because it meant, the party then thought, 'socialised medicine'. In practice, that's not how the Medicare system has worked out. Private medical practice has flourished under Medicare because it is a system for paying doctors' bills, not for employing them. Medicare has kept medical treatment affordable, but it hasn't turned doctors into virtual public servants, as was then feared. Because there is no guarantee of bulk-billing, there are still significant price signals in the system. These price signals are strong disincentives against overuse of services and against overcharging for them. The Medicare system has turned out to be a 'managed market': the best practical way to have affordable treatment and efficient service delivery.

It took some time for the Liberal Party to appreciate this marriage of affordability and choice—to realise, indeed, that it was almost the embodiment of Liberal values—but late converts can be the truest of believers. By improving Medicare through the extended safety net and the inclusion of allied-health professionals, the Howard Government was entitled to make the claim that it was the 'best friend that Medicare ever had'.

The more enthusiastic the Howard Government became about Medicare, the more the Labor Party seemed to prefer direct government service provision. If the Rudd Government ever were to take over full responsibility for health services, as it flagged prior to the 2007 election, it would almost certainly end up 'pooling' existing health funding programs (including Medicare) and placing these funds at the disposal of intermediate organisations that would purchase services for delivery to patients. This was a 2004 recommendation to the Victorian government from a major report by the Allen Consulting Group. The Rudd Government's National Health and Hospitals Reform Commission seeming preference for 'fund-holder' entities echoes that report.

Such a system would resemble, on a larger scale, divisions of general practice: government-funded bodies that largely provide services to GPs; or Aboriginal medical services, which aim to provide comprehensive primary care to Indigenous people or to people living in largely Aboriginal towns. Because they're generally small (and often quite idealistic) organisations, they tend to operate more flexibly and responsively than public hospitals. Still, resource-allocation decisions are made by officials rather than by patient choice.

A Rudd-driven, Commonwealth-run health system would most likely comprise a series of regional health organisations that would purchase services from doctors, from other health professionals and from hospitals that patients would then queue to obtain. A system such as this would be appealing to professional policy makers because it allows them to make 'rational' resource-allocation decisions. For patients, though, it would resemble the British National Health Service (NHS). Of course, the NHS is generally preferable to the US system, which does not provide universal cover. It's hard to see, though, why the need to improve public hospitals should also mean the end of Medicare and the PBS, which would ultimately disappear into giant 'pooled funds'.

The problem with health 'reform' proposals is that they usually propose to fix one problem by tackling another one. Because public hospitals' problems are allegedly caused by inadequate services outside hospitals, health 'reform' ends up proposing to tinker with private medical practice rather than to deal with over-stressed hospitals. Even though they essentially miss the point, proposals of this type are almost irresistibly attractive because they enable health departments, which are much better at lobbying than at service delivery, to sidestep any serious blame. Instead, with these sorts of recommendations, the implicit blame, to the extent that it falls anywhere, usually falls on private doctors, who are generally too busy providing services to mount an effective political counter-attack.

By contrast, the re-establishment of local hospital boards is deeply uncongenial to professional policy makers who, naturally enough, prefer to remain benevolent despots. It means that patients might be able to make personal contact with decision-makers. It means that local doctors and nurses would have reasonable access to someone who might actually be able to address their problems. Decisions might be made on the basis of how they would impact on patients rather than according to a grand design for an ideal health system or the head office–imposed budget. Experts don't normally like giving away authority, especially to members of the general public. Still, however inexpert people might be, they normally have a good sense of what's best for them.

It's claimed that local hospital boards might, for instance, try to continue providing services at their hospital that would be more efficiently provided at a larger, 'safer' one. Of course, all hospital services should be provided safely and professionally. No competent local management would run the risk of professional censure by providing an unsafe service. Instead, they would look for creative ways to provide a safe, professional service that the central bureaucracy might not be able to match. The Queensland health department, for instance, was very slow to heed whistle-blowing doctors and nurses about the alleged depredations of 'Dr Death', probably because there were so many layers of insulating bureaucracy that ought not to exist in locally managed hospitals.

Local hospital boards might decide to pay higher rates to their staff if facing a shortage. Or they might reduce rates for new staff and use the savings to provide more services. They could decide to contract out hospital management to a private operator. Most likely, they would do none of these things, but their possibility, however remote, means that locally run hospitals would not have meekly to accept whatever the health department had in mind for them. If people can be trusted to elect a parliament, why can't they be trusted with at least the capacity to buttonhole the people making decisions about their hospital?

The health system does not need fundamental restructuring or gargantuan amounts of additional funding. Hospital boards with clout are the change it needs because that change addresses the disconnect between patients and public hospital decision-makers, which is by far the system's biggest problem. Don't expect any such change, though, from Prime Minister Rudd, a former public servant who certainly hasn't kicked his own addiction to bureaucracy.

Better Dental Health

Apart from public hospitals, the other big systemic problem in health is dental treatment. The states have long provided free dental services to pensioners and other low-income people who choose to use them. Unsurprisingly, there have usually been long waiting times. In 2007, for instance, there were said to be 650,000 people on public dental waiting lists around Australia. A leaked NSW health department memo claimed that people with no teeth and no dentures who should have been seen within three months, under the program's guidelines, were waiting up to two and half years for public dental treatment at Westmead Hospital. The alternative to public dental treatment is treatment by private dentists, who might charge $125 for a half-hour consultation. Private health insurance, for the 50 per cent of the population who have ancillary cover, would typically subsidise about half of private dental costs. In part because dental treatment is either hard to access or hard to afford, about a third of country people and more than a fifth of city people have 'untreated decay' according to the Australian Institute of Health and Welfare.

The Howard Government accepted the traditional division of responsibilities and always regarded public dental treatment as the job of the states. It ended the Keating Government's program to subsidise state dental services to bring waiting lists down. This had been of limited benefit because some states had reduced their own spending. In 1995, in Queensland, notwithstanding the Keating scheme, some patients were said to have had to wait up to three years for public dental treatment. The Howard Government did make private dental treatment somewhat more affordable for those who had cover through the private health insurance rebate. Its biggest innovation in this area came just before its defeat, on my watch.

From 1 November 2007, people with chronic disease whose poor dental health was exacerbating their condition could access up to $4250 worth of Medicare-funded dental treatment in any two-year period. A Medicare rebate schedule was established that largely mirrored the long-established scheme in which private dentists provide subsidised treatment for war veterans. There had been 1.5 million Medicare-funded dental consultations by February 2009. I had always intended that this would be the precursor to making dentistry more generally available under Medicare to all people with dental problems, perhaps on referral from a GP. It had struck me as odd that Medicare should subsidise health treatment for all parts of the body except the mouth. This anomaly meant that people were frequently receiving subsidised medical treatment and subsidised drugs to palliate conditions much better tackled through unsubsidised dentistry.

Putting dentistry on Medicare in ways that maintained the universality of the system and with rebates at a level that would allow substantial bulk-billing would have been very expensive: health officials estimated the cost at up to $4 billion a year in 2007. Unfunded new spending of this magnitude could not be contemplated until the budget returns to surplus. Still, it would be the best means of ensuring that people don't miss out on essential dental treatment and is a logical development of the Medicare system. It would significantly improve Australians' overall health, with hard-to-estimate but considerable long-term economic benefits. It would enshrine the private sector as the main provider of dental services. As with Medicare more generally, it would keep price signals in the system to limit over-servicing and overcharging. Despite the budgetary cost, it's the kind of reform that conservative incrementalists should consider.

Better Schools

Although public schools are smaller, less complex institutions than public hospitals, and are less often in the news for scandalous deficiencies in service delivery, they too could benefit from being less subject to a large and unwieldy bureaucracy. Most teachers are hard-working and highly committed and there are many excellent public schools. Still, if the Teachers Federation is right, public education is being undermined because teachers are underpaid and schools are underfunded. If Kevin Donnelly, a critic with quite a different perspective, is correct:

> instead of having a robust education system committed to excellence and the highest standards of learning, we are faced with an inflexible school system suffering from provider capture, protected from competition, steeped in mediocrity and the belief that education should be used for social engineering and the promotion of political correctness.[2]

As with public hospitals, better public schools are likely to emerge when local teachers and parents have more say over how their schools are run. It's especially important to give parents a direct say in the running of schools rather than just an advisory role. Even though classroom teachers are often among the highest-minded of people, the one group to whom the interests of children are invariably paramount is those children's parents. Again, solutions involve trusting people more and relying on officials less.

Perhaps the biggest problem in education is that public educators are undervalued. Classroom teachers' salaries, in NSW public schools, for instance, start at about $53,000 and finish at about $79,000 a year. Comparatively high salaries for new graduates but comparatively low salaries for outstanding teachers who have been inspiring their students for decades are typical of centrally managed organisations. Where decision-makers don't know individuals and can't form judgments about their worth, the understandable-enough-under-the-circumstances assumption is that everyone is doing the same professional job. Thus, 'teacher quality' salary distinctions are not made on the inevitably subjective but ultimately more satisfactory basis of personal assessment but on the supposedly objective basis of time served and additional qualifications obtained. As long as teacher salaries are determined for an entire state by head office, they are always going to be somewhat higher than they should be for inexperienced or mediocre teachers but much lower than they should be for teachers with real professional flair.

Head-office control means rigid rules on class sizes and strict guidelines on variations between schools. Why should a school have to appoint new teachers from a transfer list? Why shouldn't a school be able to increase class sizes and use the savings, for instance, to employ a remedial reading teacher—or, for that matter, reduce class sizes and use local fundraising to maintain teachers' salaries? Why shouldn't a school be able to use a local builder for renovations or new construction rather than someone from the head-office list and deploy any savings on a new playground or better sports facilities? Head-office control means that fewer mistakes are made at local level but at the cost of a stultifying uniformity and suppression of initiative. Head-office control probably means that fewer mistakes are found out (because if it's happening everywhere it can't really be a 'mistake'), but it certainly doesn't mean that excellence is being fostered.

Across Australia, public schools are bedevilled by an alliance of convenience between head office and the teacher unions. To be fair, the union influence isn't always malign. In New South Wales, for instance, the Teachers Federation has maintained an old-fashioned regard for educational standards, external examinations and academically selective high schools. Still, it's also promoted uniformity between schools and high pay for everyone, on the mistaken basis that all teachers are equally good. Having very large numbers of teachers employed *at* a school rather than *by* a school is a recipe for high levels of unionism and for staff management through unions rather than through direct dealings between teachers and principals. In education, as in other sectors, high unionisation means high overall salary costs, but not high wages for the best teachers. This is very unlikely to change unless serious decision-making is devolved to the school level.

Over the past two decades, public-school parents and citizens groups have become increasingly sophisticated, mostly under the pressure of fundraising for facilities that would once have been provided via state governments. Parents who are prepared to invest their own time and money in providing air-conditioning, computers and sports equipment for their children's schools are precisely the people who should be involved in choosing the school's principal and its teachers. Although schools do not all have equally capable parent communities, all of them have parents with a vital stake in their children's futures. These parents should be more involved in making decisions about their children's education. Not to involve them because 'officials know best' is a form of snobbery that has long lost any plausible justification.

The Howard Government sought to empower local schools and their communities by paying substantial infrastructure grants directly to them on their own application (rather than through state education departments). These Investing in Our Schools grants typically paid for library extensions, school halls and playground refurbishment. They usually involved significant local co-contribution in cash or in kind. This was the first time that a Commonwealth government had directly funded individual public schools.

The next coalition government could build on this precedent by making any additional Commonwealth assistance to public schools dependent upon the establishment of school councils with the right to appoint the principal and to set priorities for the school budget. The states, assisted by the teacher unions, would furiously resist, but most parents, I'm sure, would welcome this chance to be more involved in running schools rather than just helping at them.

Giving parents and local community leaders real authority over the appointment of the principal and the approval of the school budget should, over time, ensure that schools reflect mainstream aspirations and values. Teachers who are accountable to principals who are, in turn, accountable to school communities are likely to be more professionally 'grounded' and less susceptible to avant garde fashions in curriculum and pedagogy. School councils (like hospital boards) would not solve all problems. Still, most problems should be more manageable if local people felt engaged and empowered to create their own strategies for dealing with them.

The Howard Government's other significant school reforms were standardised testing and moves towards more rigorous national curricula. Standardised testing is now largely in place, after strenuous resistance from some state governments and the teacher unions. Formerly recalcitrant state Labor governments are now working with the Rudd Government to establish national curricula, but these are unlikely to be particularly demanding or prescriptive. The English Teachers Association, for instance, has criticised the draft national English curriculum for being too insistent on 'phonics' as a way to master word skills and too traditional about what counts as literature.[3] Unless educational conservatives such as Bob Carr can reassert their influence within the ALP, it's almost inevitable that this critique from the left will be accommodated.

Although the Howard Government had a strong record in health and education, it went into the 2007 election well behind Labor as the 'party that would best handle' them. The Newspoll just prior to the 2007 election put the then government 20 points behind the ALP at handling health and Medicare and 25 points behind at handling education. By contrast, the Howard Government was 10 points ahead at handling the economy and 15 points ahead in national security.

Between 1996 and 2007, there was an 88 per cent real increase in total Commonwealth health spending, including a 48 per cent real increase in Medicare spending, a 110 per cent real increase in Pharmaceutical Benefits Scheme spending and a 204 per cent real increase in medical research spending. Between 1997 and 2005, Commonwealth health spending as a percentage of GDP increased from 3.7 per cent to 4.7 per cent. Over the same period, state health spending only increased from 2 per cent to 2.1 per cent of GDP. Private health insurance coverage increased from 34 per cent to 44 per cent of the population.[4] Most significantly, in an area where it's easier to spend money than to obtain results, life expectancy at birth increased by three years between 1996 and 2007.

Under the Howard Government, real Commonwealth spending on schools increased by 77 per cent, on vocational and technical education by 87 per cent and on universities by 13 per cent. The number of apprentices in training increased from 155,000 to 414,000, with the number in 'traditional trades' increasing from 127,000 to 181,000. The number of university students increased from 604,000 to 984,000.[5] In 2006, public school students received government funding to the tune of about $11,200 each. Students in non-government schools received government funding of about $6200 each.

To a considerable extent, the Liberal Party's prospects depend upon understanding why there was so little political dividend from the Howard Government's good work in health and education. In part, it's because parties of the left are thought to be focused on better government services, while parties of the right have been seen as more concerned with lower taxes and more efficient government. In part, it's because the Labor Party established Medicare and abolished university fees, so therefore 'owns' health and education. Despite the weak performance of the state Labor governments and the Howard Government's comparatively strong performance, it would seem that voters' attitudes, at least on these issues, are driven by the perceived purity of politicians' intentions.

Even though the extended Medicare safety net and the extension of Medicare rebates to some treatments by allied-health professionals, for instance, were important innovations, it seems that they weren't enough to demonstrate the Howard Government's wholehearted commitment to Medicare. To some extent, the ALP's critique bit: that the new safety net was a bandaid on high doctors' fees and the allied-health scheme a substitute for action on the public health system. It's not altogether surprising that voters have doubted the party's commitment to public health services and public schools, when its main policy innovations (such as the private health insurance rebate and ending the no-new-schools policy) could be portrayed as a preoccupation with providing private alternatives to them.

Advocates of smaller government can give the impression that they oppose government service delivery, even though they normally want services more effectively delivered, often by community-based or charitable organisations. The Liberal Party's reluctance to trespass on the traditional responsibilities of the states can easily be mistaken for a reluctance to provide 'national leadership' on the issues that matter to voters. In the end, significant new policy is the surest way to persuade voters that a political party takes something seriously. Provided it could be done in a fiscally responsible way, putting dentistry on Medicare could be a policy innovation big enough to allow the coalition to 'own' health.

A proposal to give the best teachers much higher salaries could similarly transform the education debate. An extra $1 billion a year could add $50,000 a year more to the pay packets of Australia's 20,000 best teachers. It could, for instance, give the top 7 per cent of Australia's 280,000 classroom teachers remuneration at about the level of members of parliament. Paying some teachers much more than others based on their experience, professional qualifications and ability to inspire their students would well accord with liberal-conservative values, even though it would mean more government spending on (mostly) public schools. Asking each school to specify how its best teachers are to be determined and how this money ought to be spent (provided that it must go to teachers but can't go to all of them) would help to encourage more initiative at the school level.

In the run-up to the next election, there will be three obstacles to big, new policies in health and education: political operators' instinct not to 'play on your opponent's turf'; oppositions' tendency to let governments lose rather than take risks themselves; and the coalition's traditional prudence with public money. On the other hand, it's hard to see the Liberal Party regaining its standing with voters on the basis of social-policy good intentions alone without specific policy innovations. It's largely true that 'governments lose elections; oppositions don't win them'. Still, first-term oppositions can't normally wait for the government to lose. New oppositions normally need some attention-grabbing policies to show voters that they have learned from losing. Even the most prudent governments should know when to spend as well as when to hoard.

7 If the 2020 Summit Had Been Fair Dinkum ...

In April 2008 the Rudd Government invited 1000 of Australia's 'best and brightest' to put forward their ideas for a better country. The 2020 Summit, co-chaired by the prime minister and the vice-chancellor of Melbourne University, came up with more than 900 ideas. Unfortunately, as someone quipped at the time, the new ideas weren't good and the good ideas weren't new. Predictably, the proposal that generated the most obvious enthusiasm from such a group was becoming a republic. When the government, twelve months later, selected only nine summit ideas for possible implementation, it should have been obvious that the enterprise had been misconceived.

Meetings only work if they have a manageable agenda and all the participants have a direct stake in the outcome. Bob Hawke's 1983 'bringing the nation together' post-election summit worked, after a fashion, because participating business and union leaders wanted to reduce unemployment by creating more viable enterprises. The problem with the 2020 Summit was its implicit assumption that every aspect of Australian life could benefit from a politically correct makeover. The summiteers took themselves too seriously and the society that shaped them not seriously enough. A more credible attempt to improve the future would have acknowledged the debt it would inevitably owe to the past.

A successful society such as Australia is unlikely to be improved by radical change. Contemporary Australia is, in most respects, a better country than it was forty years ago precisely because there have been so few radical departures from traditional values and institutions. We have built on our strengths. We've adapted and evolved. Australia today has certainly changed, but it's by no means unrecognisable as the country of our parents and grandparents.

Effective leadership is informed by the past but not ruled by it. Nostalgia certainly can't sustain a political movement. For starters, the 'good old days' were rarely as golden as retrospect makes them seem. The Australia that I grew up in was easygoing, encouraging and intoxicatingly full of life's possibilities—for me. It almost certainly was less brilliant for people who didn't live in a prosperous middle-class home on Sydney's north shore and go, surrounded by friends, from a private school to an outstanding university. I suspect that nonconformists were treated no more harshly then than today, but at least there's now less pigeonholing on the basis of gender, culture and sex. Despite greater ethnic and cultural diversity, longer working hours, 'blended' families, and a narrower consensus about values, Australia's social fabric remains strong. Most people don't cross the road to avoid a stranger in difficulty. Australians invariably try hard to be fair, especially to people they fear that they might be prejudiced against.

Since 1960, Australia's real GDP per person has more than tripled. People's possessions, such as cars, televisions and other major consumer goods, have proliferated almost beyond the wildest dreams of our grandparents. We are far more easygoing about social diversity. Aboriginal ancestry has become a badge of honour, eclipsing descent from a First Fleeter. Family breakdown has certainly increased, though, and there seems to be more mental illness, although that could be due to greater willingness to report it.

Australians are entitled to take at least a measure of pride in our country's achievements. If Australia had large and growing gaps between rich and poor, if minorities were persecuted, if we were struggling to meet an existential challenge, there'd be every reason to want fundamental change. Instead, MPs direct their passion into arguments of detail such as what constitutes a small business or how 'alcopops' should be taxed because we don't have more elemental issues to grapple with. To most Sydneysiders, the 'bikie menace' seems far more real than Islamist terrorism. Remedying past mistakes will always be important but, because so much has gone right for our country, no more important than ensuring that the future continues to reflect Australians' deepest values and most enduring achievements.

No one can say exactly what the future will hold, even by 2020, which is just eleven years away. What political leaders ought to know, though, is what to try to preserve, what to change and how change should be brought about. Notwithstanding the global financial crisis and its ramifications, the impact of climate change, and the threat of terrorism and other security challenges, Australia's natural advantages and human accomplishments should make our future as secure and as bright as anyone's. That doesn't mean, though, that success can be taken for granted.

In the late 1970s and 1980s there was some speculation that Australia might be heading down the 'Argentine path' of slow economic decline and social disintegration. Plainly, that hasn't happened, because enough people were prepared then to pay the price today of tomorrow's progress. This generation of Australians will need at least as much wisdom and courage as their recent forebears, but there's no reason to think that these virtues will be any rarer than usual.

Our fascination with change won't, of itself, make it more likely or more rapid. Come 2020, I'm confident that Australia will still have one of the world's strongest economies because the current yearning for magic-pudding economics will turn out to be short-lived. The United States will remain the world's strongest country by far, and our partnership with America will still be the foundation of our security. We will still be a 'crowned republic' because we will have concluded (perhaps reluctantly) that it's actually the least imperfect system of government. We will be more cosmopolitan than ever but perhaps less multicultural because there will be more stress on unity than on diversity. Some progress will have been made towards 'closing the gap' between Aboriginal and other Australians' standards of living (largely because fewer Aboriginal people will live in welfare villages and more of them will have received a good general education). Families won't break up any more often, because old-fashioned notions about making the most of imperfect situations will have made something of a comeback. Finally, there will have been bigger fires, more extensive floods and more ferocious storms because records are always being broken. But sea levels will be much the same, desert boundaries will not have changed much, and technology, rather than economic self-denial, will be starting to cut down atmospheric pollution.

Goodbye to Magic-Pudding Economics

Quite soon, the Rudd Government's attempts to stave off a recession by fiscal sugar hits and propping up uncompetitive businesses will come to seem like putting off the inevitable at unsustainable cost. The public, if not the government, will come to appreciate, in former British Prime Minister Jim Callaghan's words, that 'you can't spend your way out of a recession'. It might be possible, though, to reform your way through a recession, avoiding its worst ravages and setting up a long burst of future prosperity. This is how the Howard Government avoided the (admittedly less serious) tech-wreck and Asian economic meltdown recessions. This is how the Thatcher Government in Britain transformed the then moribund UK economy into the strongest in Europe. Even the Hawke Government used the recession of the early '80s to justify floating the dollar, deregulating the banks and lowering tariffs.

Neither the current revival of '70s-style union muscle flexing, with threats of retaliation against companies that outsource work or move some jobs offshore, nor the Rudd Government's union-centred industrial legislation will arrest the long-term decline in union membership. Well-educated, capable people won't subcontract to union officials the management of their economic future, especially if that means more workplace confrontation. Businesses that can't obtain the efficiencies they need to stay competitive will inevitably decline.

The involvement of Fair Work Australia might conceivably be able to mask this reality, but won't stop it.

The most pervasive economic lesson of the past thirty years is not that market capitalism has failed but that it is actually the only way to succeed in the long run, whatever short-term difficulties there may be. Every extra dollar that government spends has to be harvested from voters through higher taxes or higher borrowing and consequent pressure on interest rates. Every industry that's propped up means higher costs to consumers, who then have to cope with substandard products from suboptimal resource allocation. Government spending can anaesthetise some of the pain of adjustment, but it can't stop the need for it. Australia discovered the hard way in the 1970s and '80s that inefficient industries could not be sustained indefinitely without difficult restructuring. This lesson won't be forgotten just because, for the moment, panicked governments right around the world are pretending that there are magic wands they can wave to avoid a recession.

The real question is how much damage will be done in the process of trying to avoid the recession that is almost inevitable. My instinct is that Australians who were dismayed by the seeming harshness of the original Work Choices legislation could be much less sentimental about 'hard-won conditions' when businesses are struggling to survive and jobs are disappearing. Not everyone can be a nurse, a computer programmer or a marketing executive. Jobs for low-skilled people will be even more important in the aftermath of the downturn if Australia is to avoid very large numbers of long-term employed. After three decades of economic change, reform had almost become a dirty word, but tougher times will make the case for reform more, not less, persuasive.

The global financial crisis will make the quest for lower, simpler taxes more urgent, not less. Lower, simpler taxes will, almost inevitably, require significant spending discipline. There will be more toll roads, more congestion charges, more user-pays services and more co-contributions in the future. As long as people are receiving an improved service, and as long as the overall tax burden is actually dropping in the medium term, these will be politically defensible. New charges are only political dynamite if people think there is no new service to justify them.

Inevitably, a revenue base under pressure will mean that many good causes can't be supported or can't be supported to the extent their advocates demand. Paul Keating once declared that Australia couldn't have first-world infrastructure because we were a poor country. We can and should have better infrastructure, but it will have to be paid for with money that won't be available to spend somewhere else. The slump is almost certain to mean that people will become more conscious of the limits of government. The attitude so brilliantly satirised in Michael Costa's refrain 'I'm fat, ugly and stupid. What's the government going to do about it?' should become less prevalent.

Australia and Friends

At present, right around the world, in an international version of the tall poppy syndrome, people are inclined to revel in the problems that have befallen America. Some left-wing commentators have almost cheered the Taliban and al Qaeda because the success of its enemies will, they think, 'teach America a lesson'. The same commentators are inclined to see the global financial crisis as a salutary judgment on greed as well as a welcome sign of America's loss of economic leadership. If American leadership is bad, its absence would be worse. The alternative to American leadership would not turn out to be more enlightened leadership but no leadership at all.

There's no doubt that the wars in Iraq and Afghanistan have damaged confidence in US judgment. On the other hand, it's hard to take seriously the notion that America and its allies should not have sought out al Qaeda's havens after September 11, 2001, or ignored Saddam Hussein's defiance of supposedly binding UN resolutions.

It's easy to deride the failure to find weapons of mass destruction, even though every serious intelligence agency in the world (the French and the Russians no less than the Americans and the Israelis) thought that Saddam had them and he himself made no effort to deny them. It's right to lament the civilian deaths wrought by war, although many, perhaps more, would have died if Saddam's murderous regime had remained in place. It's easy to scoff, in a superior Western way, at 'exporting democracy' to cultures that have never known it (despite Iraqis rather taking to elections and even forming what currently looks like a stable-enough government). It's easy to ask why regime change is not imposed on other unsavoury governments, such as Zimbabwe's (which poses no commensurate threat to regional stability). Still, a weaker America means a less safe world. A humbled America means emboldened fundamentalists.

Obviously, big mistakes were made in the immediate aftermath of the Iraq invasion. Disbanding the Iraqi army meant that there were half a million unemployed men with guns. Disbanding the Baathist civil service meant that no one in authority knew how anything worked. There seems to have been a catastrophic lack of anticipation of the obvious once the immediate invasion was over. To President Bush's credit, though, he belatedly acknowledged these disasters and put in place a policy to remedy them. Iraq will need substantial Western help for some years to come, but, thanks to the surge, there's now every chance that it will come to resemble Jordan or Egypt rather than Iran or Somalia. The creation of a more-or-less functioning pluralist democracy in the Middle East would be no inconsiderable achievement and could even justify the immense sacrifices made. If this eventuates, history will be far kinder to George W Bush than his contemporaries have been.

It's not really surprising that an America that initially had trouble responding to Hurricane Katrina should mishandle the reconstruction of a whole country. It's odd, though, that the Iraq war should still be trumpeted as a monumental moral failure just when the country looks to be recovering. The 'good war/bad war' school still thinks that only the Afghanistan campaign can be morally justified, even though the Taliban are plainly unconquered. If there is a morality lesson to be drawn from these conflicts, it's not that America is the world's bully but that America and its principal allies collectively agonise over how to make the world a better place and, to their credit, believe that they have an obligation to help to resolve the world's problems. The argument is invariably over the best means to build a better world, not that it's someone else's business.

Although a safer world is in everyone's long-term interest, there's little immediate reward in being its policeman. The invasion of Iraq, for instance, certainly didn't give America or its allies access to cheap oil, which continued to be sold freely to everyone at the going international market price. It didn't give America access to strategic bases, although it might, perhaps, have helped to persuade some countries (notably Libya) that there was more to gain from cooperation than conflict. Saddam was always a much bigger threat to his immediate neighbours than he ever was to America or any of its allies apart from Israel. It was to liberate other people, to advance everyone's interests and to uphold universal values that the 'coalition of the willing' went to war in Iraq. If it's possible to engage in an altruistic war, this was it.

Australia's intervention to secure the independence of East Timor had many of the same characteristics. There was nothing in it for Australia to end Indonesia's inefficient and sometimes brutal occupation. It would have been easier to drive a hard bargain with Indonesia than with a more obviously needy fledgling state over oil and gas reserves in the Timor Sea. Australia's role in East Timor's independence put at serious risk relations with our largest neighbour. After 5000 Australian troops landed in Dili in 1999 to uphold the independence plebiscite and to restrain a murderous militia, there was a real chance of fighting with Indonesia. A historic debt of honour, a sense of solidarity with people under threat, and the desire for fair play between small countries and large drove Australia's actions.

It's not surprising that the countries doing the hardest fighting in Afghanistan are the United States, Britain and Canada. As well, the next most heavily engaged country, the Netherlands, at least since the days of William of Orange, has been the European nation closest in thinking to that of the anglosphere. By all accounts Australian troops have performed well in Afghanistan, though in small numbers. Former general Jim Molan has observed that Australia hasn't really pulled its weight either in Iraq or in Afghanistan, despite the credit we've received in Washington and London. It's wrong to expect America to be the world's policeman with only token assistance from allies. If Australia is to matter in the wider world, Australians should expect more, not less, future involvement in international security issues.

In *The Quiet American*, Graham Greene said of his subject 'I never knew a man who had better motives for all the trouble he caused'. It is often thought of America, in its dealings with the wider world, that its knowledge is scanty, its attention span short, its judgment flawed, and its actions frequently counter-productive. What can't seriously be questioned, in my view, is Americans' collective desire to be a force for good. An oft-quoted passage attributed to De Tocqueville illustrates Americans' sense that their country's greatness depends upon its goodness: 'If America ever ceases to be good it will cease to be great'. The notion that 'I am my brother's keeper' has taken particular root in America, as it has in all the English-speaking countries. It's an aspect of the West's ethical heritage that seems to be strengthening its hold over the civic culture of the anglosphere which is fastidious about the need for fairness, especially to outsiders. Along with representative democracy, the rule of law, and civic pluralism, it's a key element of the Anglo-American legacy to the wider world.

The absence of tribalism is one of the key characteristics of English-speaking cultures. The bonds between the countries of the anglosphere arise from patterns of thinking originally shaped by Shakespeare and the King James Bible, constantly reinforced by reading each other's books, watching the same movies and consuming the same international magazines. It's a solidarity based on ideas in common and even mutually shared differences of opinion rather than on race, religion or economic self-interest. These days, the books being discussed in New York or in London are as likely to have been written by an Indian or an Australian as by an American or a Briton. It's sometimes said that America and Britain are two countries 'divided by a common language'. The ability to communicate can make disagreements more obvious, but it also makes engagement far easier.

A key development is likely to be the rise of countries where English is nearly everyone's second language. English, for instance, is the mother tongue of only four of the countries of APEC, but almost everyone at APEC meetings participates in English. The rise of English shouldn't be a problem for India, but it could be for China.

Although China is likely to become even stronger in the years ahead, this may not mean much change for Australia's international relationships or foreign policy priorities. There's no reason other countries of our region could not also advance economically at much the same pace as China, or even faster. Despite its caste system, India has some key advantages—democracy and the rule of law besides the English language—and already looks as though it will become an important member of the anglosphere. Although China has had to become less repressive to accommodate more economic freedom, the long-term ability of what's still a communist government to maintain legitimacy and to satisfy popular aspirations is far from clear.

Then there's China's problem with Taiwan. Led by America, most of the world would reject any attempt by China forcibly to reclaim Taiwan. In Australia's case, this would not be choosing America over China but democracy over dictatorship. As John Howard pointed out recently, despite very important trade links and much high-level contact, 'we can never have the sort of intimate strategic relationship with China that we have with the United States because of the very different nature of the Chinese political system'.[1]

Francis Fukuyama was undoubtedly too optimistic when he declared the 'end of history' after the collapse of Soviet communism. As Islamist terrorism demonstrates, there is still a willing audience for obscurantism. It's more than possible to find a cry of rage against modernity and to harness it for retribution against the world. It's hard to imagine that the security services of the West will permanently be able to prevent nuclear terrorism in a large city with consequences much greater than those that followed September 11,

2001. Still, Western culture, especially its English-speaking version, is pervasive. Overwhelmingly, the modern world is one that's been made in English.

A Conservative Approach to Multiculturalism

A characteristic of anglosphere countries has been their openness to ideas and to people from the wider world. Since Roman times, the British Isles have absorbed successive waves of invaders followed by successive waves of refugees. For hundreds of years, Britain, and subsequently America, Canada and Australia, have been the countries of choice for people looking for a better life. Perhaps it's settler societies' intuitive sympathy for migrants; perhaps it's the self-interest of people whose prosperity has for centuries depended on world trade; perhaps it's some instinctive curiosity about other peoples and cultures. Whatever the reason, the anglosphere has uniquely welcomed migrants, not just as sojourners but as potential citizens.

In the narrative of the left, Australia was a boring outpost of the British Empire until Gough Whitlam became prime minister, formally ended the White Australia policy, instituted multiculturalism and gave Aborigines land rights. Whitlam's brief government was certainly a cultural watershed, but not everything that happened before 1972 is irrelevant and not all that happened afterwards is admirable. Australia was never quite the antipodean England of left-wing mythology. People from Africa, Asia and many of the countries of Europe were aboard the early convict fleets, as would be expected in a representative sample of London's jails. In the 1830s, after the Myall Creek massacre, white men were hanged for the murder of Aborigines. Among the Gold Rush influx were thousands of Chinese, quite a few of whom stayed after the gold they'd chased ran out. The first decade of Australia's national existence, which brought the passage of the 'White Australia' legislation, also saw our first Chinese-speaking MP, Senator Thomas Bakhap.

In one view, the formal policy of multiculturalism, which Gough Whitlam introduced and Malcolm Fraser entrenched, was producing a 'nation of tribes'. Certainly, multiculturalism gave a subsidised platform to local ethnic leaders and allowed left-wing politicians licence to deprecate traditional institutions such as the monarchy. From a different perspective, though, multiculturalism was just a new term to describe what had always been Australia's social reality: that significant numbers of people from quite different backgrounds were assimilating into Australian society in their own way and at their own pace.

As a journalist in the 1980s, I had attacked multiculturalism for eroding Australia's distinctive identity. In fact, along with other contemporary critics, I had made the mistake of underestimating the gravitational pull of the Australian way of life. I was too defensive about Western values that have turned out to have near-universal appeal. Migrants from non-European backgrounds have taken to Australia as enthusiastically as their forebears from the British Isles. This important truth first dawned on me in the campaign to keep the Crown in the Australian constitution. People with no 'ethnic' connection to the monarchy had come to appreciate its importance as a symbol of continuity and unity beyond politics.

At citizenship ceremonies in my electorate, council officers take pride in reading a list of all the countries whose citizens are becoming Australians. Far from diluting 'Australian-ness', this influx is evidence of its appeal. Far from emphasising the diversity of the Australian people, it shows people's enthusiasm to join our team. The multiplicity of languages spoken in modern Australian homes should be a source of strength and insight in dealing with other countries. The strongest and most resilient culture will turn out to be that which has emerged from the most vigorous interaction of ideas, attitudes and practices. This is why there is so little risk that the Australian version of English-speaking culture will be 'swamped', as I once feared it would be, or, indeed, that the global sway of the anglosphere is likely to diminish much.

These days, multiculturalism has largely ceased to be a battlefield in the 'culture wars'. For conservatives, diversity is no longer threatening. For the left, migrants have turned out to be too enamoured of Australia-as-it-is to be of much use in campaigns to change it.

A multiculturalism that means being relaxed about the pace at which migrants adapt is now taken for granted. It's become so uncontroversial that, sooner or later, even as a piety to be invoked on civic occasions, it will probably be dispensed with. When the former NSW premier Bob Carr replaced agencies for 'multiculturalism' with promoters of 'citizenship', he turned out to be a shrewd discerner of the national mood.

The Trouble with a Republic

One of the main arguments used against the monarchy, in the decade-long debate over removing the Crown from the constitution, was its alleged 'foreign-ness', especially to Australians who were not descended from Britons and who allegedly had no sense of kinship with the mother country. In fact, the monarchy in Australia is quite different from the monarchy in Britain. There, monarchy means the Queen and the royal family. Here, it also means governors-general and state governors. These are now always Australians who have distinguished themselves in some significant way. Although their role wouldn't be possible without a monarch to represent, it gives the Australian Crown a decidedly local flavour.

After a particularly engaging speech from NSW governor Professor Marie Bashir, a star-struck listener once observed to me that she was precisely the person you'd want as president. In fact, we're much more likely to have someone like Professor Bashir as a representative of the Crown than as the president of a republic. People who value their reputation don't normally subject themselves to the indignities of an election campaign. It's equally unlikely that a government would appoint someone with an independent mind to a presidency with the same notional powers as those currently given to the governor-general. Why would governments want to complicate their work by appointing a potential competitor for popular esteem freed from the conventions governing the Crown?

The result of moving to a republic with an elected president would be another politician in a key job. The result of a republic with an appointed president would probably be the selection of ciphers who were no threat to the government of the day. Either way, the quality of the people who are effective heads of state would likely diminish. As well, there'd be more potential for tension or even open conflict between the government and the head of state. Are the Australian people so aggravated by sharing a monarch that they'd take this risk? I doubt it very much.

Unless republicans can demonstrate that change will produce a better—or at least no worse—system of government, their cause is unlikely to prevail. So far, the 'least change' model for a republic is that devised by the late former Victorian judge and governor Richard McGarvie. McGarvie's president would have the same powers as the governor-general or governor and would be appointed by a council of the three most recently retired governors or governors-general on the recommendation of the prime minister. Even this minimalist change, however, because of the greater attention a president would inevitably receive, would be likely to produce a more assertive head of state than Australian governments are used to.

The republicans' fundamental problem, though, is that change undramatic enough to succeed is too dull to bother with. All the polls show that the public want to elect a president should Australia make such a switch. An elected president, though, would have a democratic mandate at least equal to that of a prime minister elected by the party with a majority in the House of Representatives. Just as they did in 1999, many republicans would campaign against a particular republic that they didn't regard as a safe model.

Even if a majority of Australians never again told pollsters that they supported the existing arrangements, the monarchy could survive indefinitely because people couldn't agree on a specific alternative. What's just as likely, though, is that honest republicans will eventually conclude that Australia won't change and so should make the most of what we have. After all, sharing a monarch with countries such as Canada, New Zealand and Papua New Guinea, as well as with Britain, is no great hardship. By universal agreement, the Queen has been an exemplar of duty and service. Any sense of national inadequacy that

Australia might have had should have well and truly been dispelled during the Howard years. If Australia counts for less in the world in the years ahead, people are far more likely to blame the government than the monarchy.

After the papacy, the British monarchy is Western civilisation's oldest continuing institution. Over the centuries, the monarch has evolved from absolute ruler, to head of government, to symbol of the nation. Because it is above politics, the Crown can come to symbolise the duties of government and the rights of citizens in a way that politicians can't, given the difficult decisions they have to make and the partisan rancour they arouse. Over time, the British Crown has become the Australian Crown. The governor-general, once an Englishman representing the British government, has become an Australian seeking to represent the whole people in the name of the Crown. As the evolution of the monarchy demonstrates, change is constant, but a republic is not its inevitable end point.

Good Intentions Are Not Enough

As a practical people, Australians have never been much interested in symbolism that's more trouble than it's worth. While becoming a republic is a symbolic change that could easily do harm, apologising to Aboriginal people was a symbolic change that people eventually concluded couldn't possibly hurt. Once it was reasonably clear that an apology to Aboriginal people would not justify more compensation claims, the Howard Government's refusal to make one looked like stubbornness.

At least until the second half of the twentieth century, Australian officialdom had tended to regard the presence of Aboriginal people as a liability for the nation rather than an asset. Aboriginal people were a problem to be solved rather than individuals whose heritage and culture should be taken seriously. For a long time, Australians collectively failed to extend to Aboriginal people the kind of sympathetic understanding that was readily extended, say, to the Irish and their predicament. It was generally assumed that the sooner Aboriginal people disappeared into the rest of the Australian population, the better. It was a mild enough form of racism, but it was enough to justify a formal apology.

Of itself, though, the Rudd Government's apology was a feel-good gesture. For all the paternalism of 1960s Australia, Aboriginal children were nearly all going to school and Aboriginal adults often had jobs in the real economy. In many parts of Australia today, older Aborigines can speak much better English and have had far more experience of work than their children and grandchildren. More respect for Aboriginal people and their culture has tended to produce a new double standard: Aboriginal children are not really expected to attend school unless it satisfies what are imagined to be their cultural sensitivities, and Aboriginal adults are not really expected to work outside Aboriginal organisations.

The gap between Aborigines' and other Australians' life expectancy is more the result of different lifestyles than different access to health services. Generally speaking, Aboriginal townships now have better health facilities than other settlements of similar size. Aboriginal people's high incidence of chronic disease, substance abuse and domestic violence are a function of unemployment, lack of education and very isolated living, not official neglect. In fact, poor Aboriginal health indicators are actually not so very different from those of other people living in similar circumstances. These won't substantially change until Aboriginal people have similar educational attainments and employment outcomes to those of other Australians.

In a country that's long been officially committed to cultural diversity as almost the highest civic good, it's hard for some to accept that Aboriginal culture was irrevocably changed by the arrival of the First Fleet. In the end, though, culture is a product of history and experience. It expresses a people's deeper values and belief systems. Today's Aborigines retain a strong sense of connectedness to family, community and land. To a considerable extent, this has come to characterise most Australians. In addition, I suspect that the laconic, even fatalistic aspect of the Australian character (perhaps most evident in the military) owes much to the interaction of settlers with Aborigines. Still, it's self-evident that today's Aborigines generally have more in common with their contemporary fellow Australians than with their hunter-gatherer forebears.

Noel Pearson says that there's no conflict between being Aboriginal and fully participating in modern Australia. If the Aborigines of Cape York, for instance, are to have similar economic outcomes to those of other Australians, they will develop, says Pearson, 'orbits' that might take in Weipa, Cairns, Townsville and Brisbane—or New York and London, for that matter—as well as their traditional country. This means obtaining the best possible education in English in high-quality local primary schools and then in academically rigorous boarding schools before working or studying wherever the best opportunities present. Pearson warns that governments won't indefinitely fund settlements with no economic base and that Aboriginal people themselves will eventually have to sustain them, much as retirees and holidaymakers sustain many other remote communities on the coast or in the bush.

If the fundamental object of government policy is to preserve Aboriginal culture it will fail. Only Aboriginal people can do that. Government cannot ask a people, in WEH Stanner's memorable phrase, 'to un-be'. On the other hand, neither can it determine the extent to which people see themselves as 'Aboriginal' or as 'Australian'. It would be just as wrong for a government to try to keep people in a box marked 'Aboriginal' as it would be to try to transfer them to another box marked 'Australian'.

Government's job is to try to equip Aboriginal people to participate in wider Australian society. Building more Aboriginal housing in places where there are no jobs, especially at rents far below the public-housing standard of 25 per cent of household income, makes people's lives easier in the short term but, in the long term, traps them in welfare villages. It's important to ensure that native-title land can serve as an economic asset as well as a spiritual one. It's important to give Aboriginal people in remote areas a chance to have individual rather than collective title. Most of all, though, it's essential that rents be realistic and that payment be enforced so that moving to seek employment can start to make more economic sense.

Australians of earlier times might have been condescending about Aboriginal people, but at least some had a strong sense of duty towards them. The unfairly maligned missionaries may have had little time for Aboriginal beliefs, but many of them spent their entire adult lives in the service of Aboriginal people. Life in remote places was more of a hardship then than now. Today's public servants flying in and out of Aboriginal towns on short-term contracts might be much more deferential to an idealised version of Aboriginal culture, but they're hardly more committed than their missionary predecessors.

Under the ideology of self-determination, an exaggerated respect for Aboriginal culture has coexisted with a kind of abandonment of Aboriginal people. Throughout remote Australia, in the name of self-management and out of what's thought to be cultural sensitivity, Aboriginal people are expected to serve on management committees for the provision of the full range of municipal, commercial and health services. This is a task that would frustrate and overwhelm the residents of most Australian suburbs, let alone people with little education and poor command of English. The result is ferocious internal politics, entrenched nepotism and generally substandard services normally delivered by outsiders with a mixed level of commitment to the places they're working in. For all its good intentions, self-determination has set up Aboriginal people to fail.

The provision of high-quality educational, health and other services to Aboriginal people requires the long-term commitment of first-class teachers, doctors and officials. The Howard Government's appointment (as part of the intervention) of resident 'government business managers' to live in remote NT towns and to have oversight of all government services there was a step in this direction. It was an attempt to re-create in the modern era and with modern attitudes something of the sustained commitment to advancing Aboriginal people's interests that had existed in mission times. The Rudd Government's announcement of a Remote Area Health Corps builds on work done by the previous government to make working in Aboriginal medical services as professionally prestigious as working in a big teaching hospital.

Working in remote towns shouldn't be seen as a hardship that junior teachers, doctors, nurses, policemen and public servants have to endure for a few months before moving back to more congenial places. At the very least, a posting to a remote town should be as professionally important and, therefore, as potentially sought after as, say, postings to active service for military personnel. It's also important for politicians and other policy makers, as far as possible, to become as familiar with the real life of Aboriginal towns as they have been with the rhetoric of social justice.

Of course Aboriginal children should be expected to attend school, and their parents should be fined under truancy laws if they don't; Aboriginal adults should attend work programs and lose social security benefits if they don't; Aboriginal housing should be maintained, with rent paid and unauthorised residents evicted. It will be hard to know whether normal community standards are being observed, though, unless senior officials actually live in these towns. If these places are not good enough for officials to live in and to raise their families in, they're unlikely to be very satisfactory for anyone else.

Environmentalism Might Hurt the Environment

One consequence of Aboriginal habitation has been the impact of 'firestick farming'. This is an example of human impact on the environment leading, it seems, to a more sparsely vegetated and perhaps drier continent over the course of the last 50,000 years. Without regular burning over thousands of years, it seems that Australia could have had somewhat different flora and fauna and lusher vegetation with different rates of water runoff. There's no doubt that humans can have a big impact on the immediate environment and a significant impact on micro-climates. Whether humans have had a significant impact on the climate as a whole is much less clear.

Climate change is a relatively new political issue, but it's been happening since the earth's beginning. The extinction of the dinosaurs is thought to have been associated with major climate change. The last ice age is a more recent period when the world's climate was quite different from today. In Roman times, grapes were widely grown in Britain. In medieval times, Greenland supported agriculture. During the mini-ice age, from the 1500s to the 1800s, people skated and ice fairs were held on the River Thames. Of course, these climatic changes had little or nothing to do with human activity.

As Australia's leading geologist, Professor Ian Plimer, says in his new book, *Heaven and Earth: Global Warming—the Missing Science*:

> climates far warmer than the late 20th century warming existed before industrialisation and human emissions of carbon dioxide. The notion that climate change is tied only to human activity with known atmospheric and ocean feedbacks is a simple and erroneous explanation of modern and ancient climates ... To argue that modern climate is driven by slight changes in a trace gas in the atmosphere requires many non-scientific leaps of faith.[2]

The continuing drought in south-eastern Australia, on some measures more severe than the Federation drought, has predisposed people to believe in harmful, human-induced climate change. On the other hand, several cold winters in Europe and in North America have made the concept of 'global warming' less plausible. Perhaps this explains the shift in polemical terminology to the less prescriptive 'climate change'.

Atmospheric concentrations of carbon dioxide have significantly increased since the spread of industrialism, but it seems that noticeable warming has only taken place between the 1970s and the 1990s. It's quite likely that increased carbon dioxide in the atmosphere has had some effect on climate, but debate rages among scientists over its extent and relative impact given all the other factors at work. It sounds like common sense to minimise human impact on the environment and to reduce the human contribution to increased atmospheric-gas concentrations. It doesn't make much sense, though, to impose certain and substantial costs on the economy now in order to avoid unknown and perhaps even benign changes in the future. As Bjorn Lomborg has said: 'Natural science has undeniably shown us that global warming is man-made and real. But just as undeniable is the economic science, which makes it clear that a narrow focus on reducing carbon emissions could leave future generations lumbered with major costs, without major cuts in temperatures'.[3]

About 80 per cent of carbon dioxide emissions are caused by intensive agriculture, the use of motor cars and generating electricity from fossil fuels. A substantial reduction in emissions will require less efficient forms of agriculture, big changes in lifestyle and higher power costs. Many climate change protagonists are also committed to ending what they see as wasteful consumerism. That's a perfectly legitimate point of view. Still, the correlation between what's presented as a scientific consensus on the need for lower emissions and standard new-left prejudice against economic growth is suspiciously neat.

If failure quickly to reduce carbon emissions really was likely to submerge Pacific islands, flood Bangladesh and turn bread baskets into deserts, it would be folly not to act urgently. It's hard to take climate alarmists all that seriously, though, when they're as ferociously against the one proven technology that could reduce electricity emissions almost to zero, nuclear power, as they are in favour of urgent reductions in emissions. For many, reducing emissions is a means to achieving a political objective they could not otherwise gain.

Of course, suspect motives don't de-legitimise good policy. The fact that a green fringe would like Australians to live like the Amish doesn't of itself invalidate reducing carbon emissions as prudent insurance against possible future harm. As always, the best course of action should be determined through sensible cost-benefit analysis.

The Howard Government proposed an emissions trading scheme because this seemed the best way to obtain the highest emission reduction at the lowest cost. Issuing licences would enable government to cap overall emissions. Allowing trade would advantage the least polluting businesses over the most polluting ones. As licences would be valuable assets, businesses would have a strong incentive to compete in becoming environmentally efficient. On the other hand, artificially created markets could be especially open to manipulation. Issuing taxi licences in Sydney, for instance, has certainly created a market, but not a very competitive one, and the main beneficiaries seem to have been licence holders rather than consumers. For this reason, many now think that a carbon charge scheme directed at the least environmentally efficient producers would be simpler and fairer than an emissions trading system.

Another big problem with any Australian emissions reduction scheme is that it would not make a material difference to atmospheric carbon concentrations unless the big international polluters had similar schemes. Australia accounts for about 1 per cent of global carbon dioxide emissions. At recent rates of growth, China's increase in emissions in about a year could match Australia's entire carbon dioxide output. Without binding universal arrangements, any effort by Australia could turn out to be a futile gesture, damaging local industry but making no appreciable dent in global emissions.

The Rudd Government's changes to the proposed emissions trading scheme, which now largely mirrors the Howard Government's once-reviled model and timetable, suggest a belated recognition of its logistical complexity. Imposing new direct costs on the power, transport and agricultural sectors may not, in fact, be the best way to limit carbon dioxide emissions. In a recent speech, for instance, Malcolm Turnbull has said that re-vegetation, more energy-efficient buildings, and further research into geothermal and tidal power could lead to greater carbon dioxide emission reductions than the proposed ETS.

Direct measures that improve the efficiency of cars, encourage the use of renewable energy such as domestic solar power, promote recycling with urban rainwater tanks, create carbon sinks on grazing land, and make coal burning less polluting are all worthwhile. Cars that use less petrol, electricity bills that are potentially lower, dam water that goes further, and land that's better managed are changes that make sense on their merits. They don't do the damage to export industries that is inherent in an unreciprocated emissions trading scheme or even a carbon charge.

Technology is our indispensable ally in reducing carbon emissions while preserving living standards. Australia's future is unlikely to be greener if that means it will necessarily be poorer too. Australians will continue to tell pollsters that they want action for a cleaner environment, but they are unlikely to support policy changes that they think might make daily life harder or much more expensive.

Kings in Their Own Cars

Fears about climate change have helped to reinforce longstanding ambivalence about the private car, even though it's hard to imagine most Australians readily coping without access to one. In a more closely settled country, like England, with excellent (if expensive) public transport, it's easy enough to live without a car. In two years at Oxford, for instance, I never missed the car because all the amenities of that fabled city were within walking or easy cycling distance and anything in London was only a train and tube ride away.

Australia is very different. We have twenty-one million people spread over an area about the size of continental Europe. Sydney (along with other Australian cities) is different too. Sydney has four million people, mostly living in detached houses, in an area larger than London with its ten million plus. Short of attaining London-style population densities, it's fanciful to imagine that Sydney could have a London-style public transport system. London-style population density, though, would not only mean much more medium- and high-density living; it would also put far more pressure on the health of Sydney's waterways with much less green space.

Most people would be happy to use public transport if it went from near where they are to near where they wanted to go, quickly and regularly. On the other hand, busy people are understandably reluctant to use public transport if it means planning their day around once-an-hour bus timetables. In Australia's big cities, public transport is generally slow, expensive, not especially reliable and still a hideous drain on the public purse. Part of the problem is inefficient, overmanned, union-dominated, government-run train and bus systems. Mostly, though, the problem is the economics of public transport in a suburban metropolis. Mostly, there just aren't enough people wanting to go from a particular place to a particular destination at a particular time to justify any vehicle larger than a car, and cars need roads.

It's easy to understand the official prejudice against private transport. Cars are expensive and polluting. Roads are expensive and can blight the urban environment. People who can afford to live in the inner city or on a train line, or who have access to a cab charge that someone else pays for, often puzzle over others' attachment to their own car and passion to drive. They underestimate the sense of mastery that many people gain from their car. The humblest person is king in his own car. Drivers choose the destination, the route, the time of departure, the music that's played and whether to have company. Women, especially, tend to value the sense of security that a car can give. For people whose lives otherwise run largely at the beck and call of others, that's no small freedom. It should not be underestimated or sneered at by senior policy makers who are more accustomed to getting their own way.

For too long, policy makers have ranked motorists just above heavy drinkers or smokers as social pariahs. Motorists are not self-indulgent burdens on the community, too unfit to ride a bike or too selfish to catch a bus. They're citizens going to work, doing the shopping, taking the kids to school or visiting their relatives. They should not be subjected to wildly inconsistent speed limits, oppressive penalties for minor transgressions and, above all, streets designed for the traffic of fifty years ago or motorways that go nowhere.

The Howard Government received little credit for the new roads it directly funded (such as, in New South Wales, massive improvements to the Hume Highway) and part-funded via tax concessions (such as Sydney's Eastern Distributor, the M5 East and the M7). The Rudd Government's recession-busting infrastructure list has been light on new and upgraded roads, especially in metropolitan areas, reflecting policy makers' anti-road hang-ups. In a first–world country, Brisbane, Sydney, Canberra, Melbourne and Adelaide should long ago have been linked by a four-lane highway. Within our major cities, there should long have been connected-up arterial expressways.

Sydney, for instance, should fill the gaps between the CBD and the M4 at Strathfield, the expressway at Hornsby and the M2, and the M5 and the expressway at Heathcote. There should be a link between the northern beaches and the city and between the western suburbs and Port Botany. Of course, new major roads would quickly become congested in peak times, but that would largely be due to the additional economic activity that they'd generate.

New roads would provide space for dedicated bus lanes, so they'd mean better public as well as private transport. They should also be coupled with wide shoulders for bikes. Indeed, it should be a standard condition of new roads that they make space for bikes, new housing developments that there are footpaths and new commercial buildings that they have lockers and showers for people who walk or ride to work. Modern technology means that road tunnels can readily substitute for suburb-dividing traffic canyons. Provided they were built at competitive cost, major new roads (along with other economic infrastructure) would be a very good policy response to the economic downturn. Instead, the Rudd Government is more likely to opt for more union-friendly infrastructure investment (in underused railways or metros, for instance).

The Evolving Family

No look into the possible or the desirable future can neglect some consideration of the evolution of the family. The families that most of us are familiar with are often sole-parent or blended ones rather than the idealised version with two biological parents and lots of children living in happy proximity to grandparents and cousins. There are more single people too in our extended families. Families that conform to the traditional norm also have their share of tensions and antagonisms. Still, everyone comes from a family of sorts and nearly everyone craves the deep communion with at least one other person that a spousal relationship should bring. People can change and grow apart, wrestle with sexual ambivalence, or find marital fidelity hard to maintain without losing their respect for the traditional ideal of marriage.

The fact that the divorce rate has increased from about 10 per cent to about 40 per cent in the past two generations is not really so surprising. Nor is the fact that people frequently live together before making a formal commitment to each other. It reflects the social changes of the past century much more than it signifies a collapse of moral standards. Young people reach sexual maturity earlier but leave school much later and often spend years in higher or further education. It takes time to establish the independent households that most newly married people now expect.

A hundred years ago, most people married their first love at about twenty and lived to be about fifty. These days, people typically marry their third or fourth love at about thirty and live to be about eighty. It's not realistic to expect most young adults in this hypersexualised age to live chastely for many years outside marriage. Even if people's expectations of their partners and spouses were much less high, longer lives would tend to mean more potential exposure to the rocks on which marriages often founder. People have not so much abandoned traditional mores as found that the old standards don't so readily fit the circumstances of their lives.

Regretting the rate of family breakdown is not the same as casting moral aspersions on everyone whose marriage has failed. If a marriage is making the life of a spouse or child wretched, it may best be ended. Still, many marriages are entered into with unrealistic expectations of future bliss. Many marriages end because spouses aren't prepared for the give and take that a lasting relationship requires. The social pressures that might once have trapped people in destructive relationships have all been reversed. I doubt that the human propensity for selfishness, coldness and unfaithfulness has much increased. It's just that, these days, separation and divorce no longer seems to be quite the final resort when faced with marital stress.

The Family Law Act of 1975 substituted one year's separation for the traditional grounds of divorce: cruelty, adultery or abandonment. It certainly helped many people to escape from destructive relationships. On the other hand, it also led to an explosion in the number of children growing up in fatherless or motherless households. Most children are pretty resilient and manage to cope with loss in their own way. Still, only the most starry-eyed member of the Woodstock generation would maintain that a parent's self-fulfilment readily justifies depriving children of living with both a mother and a father, especially when the children are young. Most people who have lived with the consequences of family breakdown have grown out of being 'non-judgmental' about the choices people make, however sympathetic they might be towards the individuals making them.

The Howard Government established a network of family relationship centres as an alternative to the courts for couples seeking a divorce. In helping people to settle their disputes more amicably, these centres actually taught some couples the skills necessary to stay together. For at least some members of the former government, these centres were an important official acknowledgment of the human cost of divorce and a small but unmistakeable sign that society should not be indifferent to the fate of marriages. Some American states have created a new category of marriage. As well as a marriage that can be ended after a brief separation, these states now allow couples who choose to do so to enter into a marriage that's harder to end. It's often called a 'covenant' marriage but is really more akin to the pre-Lionel Murphy Matrimonial Causes Act concept of marriage.

The last thing that anyone should want is to seek to chain together people who are bringing out the worst in each other. On the other hand, if the law is to be the moral teacher that the advocates of 'better-behaviour' legislation think it should be, why not establish another type of marriage that people could enter if they think that their commitment really should be 'till death us do part'? Certainly, if the law is to establish a new type of legally recognised relationship for gay couples, it might also manage to enshrine once more, for those who want it, a type of marriage that approximates to the Christian ideal.

I could turn out to be mistaken, of course, about the likely future of family life, the significance of climate change, the development of economic policy, Australia's international environment, social integration, the monarchy, and Aboriginal advancement. Even so, I doubt that Australia in 2020 will seem alien to someone who'd been out of the country for the previous decade. Much stays the same even in the midst of huge changes. Short of an economic catastrophe, powerful external threat or improbable domestic revolution, the changes of the coming decade will be modest and incremental. That won't mean that Australia has become dull or its politicians ineffective. It will just mean that we've continued to be more successful at giving citizens a decent life than most other nations.

Postscript: Days from Hell

Everyone has days from hell. The difference between a politician's very bad day and most people's is that the worse a politician's troubles are, the more likely they are to be on national TV. My day from hell was 31 October 2007. The papers reported that I'd 'abused' dying anti-asbestos campaigner Bernie Banton by suggesting that his protest outside my office the previous day had been a political stunt. Even though I'd phoned Banton to apologise while on the way to a health policy launch in Melbourne (and he had been good enough to acknowledge that he'd also been intemperate about me), I spent the morning publicly saying sorry for impugning the motives of a Labor hero.

Although the prime minister arrived punctually, he then spent nearly half an hour shaking hands, made an especially exuberant speech and answered media questions at length while I stood beside him worrying about the time and wanting to get away. The event ran half an hour over schedule, which meant that I was eventually half an hour late into Canberra for a nationally televised debate with the shadow health minister. At the photo shoot afterwards, I said 'that's bullshit' to Nicola Roxon's accusation that I could have been on time if I'd tried. The day-that-could-hardly-get-worse deteriorated even further when the Tasmanian government announced new obstacles to transferring to the Commonwealth the ownership of the Mersey hospital. The finale, a *Lateline* debate against a gloating Julia Gillard (who was herself, subsequently, late for an election debate), at least prompted a rare Tony Jones compliment for having had the guts to turn up.

A few days later, while visiting Westmead hospital, a formidable-looking nurse approached—not, to my relief, with a complaint about Work Choices: 'I just want you to know that in our house "bullshit" is not a swear word and if I had been spoken to like that I would have told her to f—k off'. For me, this was a rare encouraging moment in a campaign that often seemed to go from bad to worse.

'You had a lousy campaign' was one of the reasons my colleagues gave for urging me not to stand in the leadership ballot after the 2007 election. Others were that I was 'too hardline' or 'too close to Howard'. Six years' hard work in parliament as Leader of the House of Representatives, nine years as a minister managing fraught portfolios, and regular intellectual advocacy on behalf of a sometimes rhetorically challenged government seemed to count for little or nothing. It was, of course, a potent reminder that you're only as good as your most recent performance and that mistakes are remembered more than achievements.

Memories of the campaign will inevitably fade. By contrast, a reputation for being strident doesn't necessarily dissipate with time. In particular, there was my colleagues' judgment that I was 'too Catholic' on some sensitive issues. In some ways, this was an odd perception. A somewhat chequered past meant that I could never be sanctimonious about personal behaviour. How could I be judgmental about others, given my own failures to live up to ideals of good conduct?

As an ambitious politician, I had never had the slightest intention of becoming a morals campaigner. Shortly after becoming health minister, though, I'd been asked to justify Medicare funding for up to 75,000 abortions every year. It was a question that compelled an answer. The first instalment, delivered in March 2004 as a speech entitled 'The Ethical Responsibilities of a Christian Politician', distinguished between deploring the frequency of abortion and trying to re-criminalise it. In a speech shortly after the 2004 election I had even endorsed, at least as an improvement on the current situation, Bill Clinton's observation that abortion should be 'safe, legal and rare'.

The subsequent parliamentary debate over the abortion drug RU486 exposed a post-Christian parliament's reservations about the suitability of Catholics for certain jobs. It also revealed a new consensus, even among MPs, that Australia's abortion rate was far too high. I had never supported any move to re-criminalise abortion, because that would have stigmatised millions of Australian women who had taken what they thought was the 'least worst' option in a difficult situation. Instead, at my instigation, the Howard Government had introduced a new helpline to give more support to women facing an unexpected pregnancy. It seemed to be the best way to nudge the abortion rate down without affecting women's right to choose. Even so, it was enough to make me the 'Captain Catholic' of Australian politics.

Like the other tags that have been applied to me over the years, such as 'arch-monarchist' and 'Howard's head-kicker', this one could lose currency as circumstances change. In the meantime, it might not hurt to have another senior coalition frontbencher taking Christian concerns seriously. Kevin Rudd certainly thought that a Christian vote mattered, as his first essay for *The Monthly* claiming Dietrich Bonhoeffer as his role model demonstrated. Electorates with a comparatively high number of church-going Christians recorded stronger-than-average swings to Labor in 2007. If the Australian Christian Lobby is right, these voters could swing back to the coalition as the Labor Party's secular humanist instincts reassert themselves over, for instance, foreign aid for third-world abortions. Christian voters are likely to find Rudd's 'I didn't like it, but I couldn't stop it' response on this issue particularly lame. As well, given some Liberals' uncertainties about the party's direction, it's good that there are still senior frontbenchers who might be thought of as keepers of the conservative conscience.

This book is not a history of the Howard Government, but it does canvass what can be learnt from its experience. It's not a political-science tract, but it has explored the values and instincts that drive the Liberal Party. It's not a party manifesto, although there are new policy ideas here that are consistent with our traditions. It's not a volume of memoirs, although it obviously has drawn on my personal experience. Last, it's not a job application, because I expect that the existing team will lead the party to the next election. I hope it might serve to rally my fellow Liberals and to persuade others that politics is a venture worth engaging in.

For years I had said, somewhat glibly, that politics is a vocation. It takes losing government to appreciate what that really means. Only someone reconciled to living without all the trappings of success really has a vocation. Opposition naturally strips away most of the cheer squad, leaving just the stark question: are you still willing to serve?

As the German sociologist Max Weber has noted, politicians have to understand the comparative smallness of their own role in the unfolding of events and the inevitability of failure in some of their most treasured projects. Only those who still think it's worth the hazard have grasped the true calling of politics.

Defeat can be a better teacher than success. It certainly helped to form John Howard's political character. Had he been elected in 1987, he would have been a different and, I suspect, lesser prime minister. Of course, only a masochist would be indifferent to success. Still, former senior members of the Howard Government who survive the experience of opposition should be more sensitive and ultimately more formidable politicians because they will have become better acquainted with struggle.

It's time for battlelines to be drawn. The Liberal Party certainly has to maintain its credibility as the best party to manage the economy, but it also has to be clear about the society it wants. A society where politicians can less easily make excuses for failing to address problems; where more responsive health and education services are available to everyone; where government is in sympathy with individuals and families trying to get ahead; and where the values and the institutions that have stood the test of time are respected should always be the goal to which our party is committed.

Afterword: A Week Really Can Be a Long Time in Politics

On 24 July 2009, in an op-ed piece for *The Australian*, I said that the coalition should not oppose the government's emissions trading legislation because it was a fight we would not win. It was a way to support Malcolm Turnbull's leadership while also putting on the public record my deep reservations about an ETS and dismay at a debate conducted in terms of 'believers' and 'deniers'.

Over the following few weeks, some of my strongest backers took me to task, as they saw it, for trying to win votes rather than to do good. At a dinner in my own electorate hosted by the local Liberal Party to promote *Battlelines*, the argument that the coalition should not try to save the country from Mr Rudd's emissions tax was all but howled down. Their counter-argument was the aphorism attributed to Paul Keating: that bad policy would always turn out to be bad politics. I thought then, as I think now, that something has to be done about climate change. What gradually dawned on me, though, as I reflected on these rebuffs, was that action on climate change didn't have to mean this ETS at this time.

Notoriously, as it subsequently turned out, at a Liberal Party dinner at Beaufort in country Victoria on 30 September, I said that the so-called settled science of climate change was 'crap' but that it was a difficult issue for the coalition. After my comment was reported in the local paper, the Rudd Government gleefully leapt on this attempt to justify Turnbull's position to a hostile audience as evidence of a hopelessly confused opposition.

In fact, it was on that trip that I concluded that the politics of this issue really had changed. Opinion polls were by then showing that, although a majority of Australians supported an ETS, an even larger majority wanted more information about it and about half were opposed to an ETS before the rest of the world decided its position at the Copenhagen conference in December.

Earlier that day, in the course of a shadow cabinet discussion in Adelaide, it had become obvious that the Nationals would oppose the ETS legislation regardless of the position of its coalition partner. It was also apparent by then that a substantial number of Liberal Party backbenchers were hostile to the legislation and that some of them would cross the floor of the parliament in defiance of any directive to support it.

On the charter flight from Mt Gambier to Bendigo and the subsequent drive to Beaufort, my colleague, former speaker David Hawker, explained the difficult position of regional Liberal MPs confronting a bush revolt against what country people saw as just another new tax. Farmers were used to adapting to climate change, he said. It was climate change policy that could kill their businesses. A long phone conversation with Nick Minchin during the Comcar trip back to Melbourne the next day crystallised my new thinking: voting for the legislation would fracture the coalition and split the Liberal Party; opposing the legislation would give the coalition the chance to campaign against Labor's giant new tax on everything.

An obvious difficulty, though, was the view of the party leader. Over the next two months, I had many opportunities to put this to Turnbull: in phone conversations, in shadow cabinet discussions, during a meal at his home and even on morning bike rides around the lake in Canberra. Malcolm was easy to talk to but impossible to persuade that this was becoming a slow motion train wreck. His political credibility, he said, meant that the party had to support an amended ETS that protected farmers, consumers and exporters. Our only leverage over the government, he said, was the prime minister's vanity to be the one world leader at the Copenhagen conference to have a legislated emissions scheme. Malcolm was determined that the negotiations over an amended bill must succeed. I argued that it would be best for the coalition if they were to fail.

This issue came to a head at a shadow cabinet meeting in Canberra on Tuesday 24 November. By then, my view was that the ETS could be characterised as a giant tax: creating a huge slush fund, providing massive handouts and spawning a vast bureaucracy. It would be crazy for the Liberal Party to be complicit in a change of this nature. After a lengthy discussion, the shadow cabinet decided, fourteen to six it was subsequently reported, to back the recommendation supported by the leader.

In the coalition party room, thirty-five speakers (by the leader's count) supported the shadow cabinet recommendation, while forty opposed it. Turnbull then added the shadow cabinet numbers to declare that the recommendation to back the amended legislation had been carried by forty-nine votes to forty-six. It certainly hadn't been carried, though, in the party room, where shadow cabinet members are not allowed to speak. The meeting broke up in disorder after Malcolm called the result (as he saw it); it reconvened after he was persuaded that matters couldn't be left hanging; and it broke up again in even greater disorder after he rejected Minchin's compromise proposition. This was to accept the negotiated amendments but to refer the amended bill to a Senate committee for further scrutiny and then to deal with it in February after the Copenhagen conference.

In interviews the following morning, I did my best to defend Turnbull and said that the opposition had won very significant concessions from the government. At about 11 a.m., Turnbull called a snap party room meeting to consider a motion that had been lodged the previous evening to declare the leadership vacant. Two hours later, with only the former Howard Government minister Kevin Andrews a declared candidate, the spill motion failed forty-eight votes to thirty-five. It was hardly a decisive vote of confidence in the leader. In my view, Malcolm shouldn't have authorised a negotiation that made the coalition effective co-sponsors of the ETS; shouldn't have persisted with a recommendation that was so obviously divisive; and shouldn't have claimed vindication when his authority had so obviously eroded. He had striven for a policy he believed in, but his admirable determination had foundered on the right of the party room to be taken seriously.

That afternoon, I discussed with colleagues the option of resigning from the front bench if Turnbull did not reconsider his support for the ETS legislation. I'd discussed the party's ETS dilemma a number of times with John Howard but deliberately did not raise this option with him. Much as I have always respected his judgment, I didn't want anyone else's fingerprints on my decision.

The next morning, on Thursday 26 November, Minchin and I decided that we would both see Turnbull after question time to request that he adopt the earlier compromise proposal. After a discussion that was courteous but predictable, I told Malcolm that I could no longer support the policy and was therefore resigning from the front bench. In the next twenty-four hours, two more shadow cabinet ministers and seven other office holders resigned their positions. Even then, the objective was to change the policy rather than to change the leadership. However, Malcolm's response—a defiant press conference attack on colleagues who wanted, he claimed, to 'do nothing' on climate change—meant that a change of leadership was a real possibility.

At about lunch time on Friday, along with nine colleagues, I wrote to the party whip requesting another meeting to spill the leadership. I told the media that my objective in running was to stop the ETS legislation going through the parliament before Copenhagen and then to heal the party's wounds. But if another candidate might be a more unifying leader, I said that I would be happy to defer.

Since Peter Costello had left the parliament, polls had shown that the shadow treasurer, Joe Hockey, was consistently the most popular alternative Liberal Party leader. Ringing around my colleagues over the weekend, most seemed to have given up on Malcolm, but many thought that Joe was our best option and assumed that he would be the candidate. Climbing into bed late on Sunday night, I couldn't decide whether to be disappointed or relieved that the next leader would not be me.

On the morning of Monday 30 November, though, Joe was still debating with himself whether to run and, in particular, how to handle the ETS legislation. At 11 a.m., 4 p.m. and again at 6 p.m. there were long meetings to thrash this out. Eventually, he decided that, if the legislation could not be referred to a Senate committee, there would have to be a free vote in the parliament for Liberal members and senators. He had tried hard to devise a way to keep the party together, but being officially undecided on something as important as this, I thought, just would not do. Therefore I declared just after 7 p.m. that I would certainly be a candidate regardless of whether anyone else ran. It was important for ETS opponents to have a candidate who shared their view.

Despite frantic phone calling and corridor conferencing, even the most experienced 'numbers men' thought that I would fall a few votes short. A tremor ran through the party room on the morning of Tuesday 1 December when the most electorally popular man in the party got the least votes in the first ballot, setting up a final contest that Malcolm would find hard to win. Thank God, I thought, fighting down nerves, that I had scribbled a few notes on what I might say if I won. Just as well, too, that Kevin Andrews, who normally sits beside me in the party room, had had the presence of mind to have ready a draft motion on the ETS legislation to be put to the party room in a secret ballot. Its success, fifty-four votes to twenty-nine, gave great authority to the new policy and helped to ensure that only two senators—Judith Troeth and Sue Boyce—of the seven or eight who had earlier spoken in favour of the bills crossed the floor to vote with the government.

As things stand, there will almost certainly be a climate change election. It won't just be about climate change, but that will be the totemic issue. The government will say that lifting the price of carbon is necessary to help the environment. That might be the case one day, but certainly not now. The challenge is to find ways to improve the environment without a great big new tax.

When Winston Churchill drove to Buckingham Palace in the dark days of 1940 to accept the king's commission, he felt that his whole life had been but a preparation for this moment, or so he recounts in his memoirs. This is not wartime Britain. And I am certainly not Winston Churchill. Still, I feel well equipped to take on the leadership of the party in what are testing times for the conservative side of politics.

4 December 2009

Appendix: A Bill to Amend the Constitution

The Parliament of the
Commonwealth of Australia

HOUSE OF REPRESENTATIVES

Presented and read a first time

Constitution Alteration (Commonwealth and State Powers) Bill

(Mr Abbott)

A Bill for an Act to alter the Constitution to enable a more effective exercise of Commonwealth power in areas of responsibility shared with the States.

The Parliament of Australia, with the approval of the electors, as required by the Constitution, enacts:

1 Short title

This Act may be cited as the *Constitution Alteration (Commonwealth–State Cooperation) Act*.

2 Commencement

This Act commences on the day on which it receives the Royal Assent.

3 Schedule

The Constitution is altered as set out in the Schedule.

Schedule 1—Amendment of the Constitution

1 At the end of section 51

Add:

"51A The Parliament shall, subject to this Constitution, have power to make laws for the peace, order and good government of the Commonwealth with respect to any other matters in addition to those listed in section 51, provided that a proposed law within the meaning of this section must be passed by both Houses on two occasions—not less than six months apart."

2 At the end of the first paragraph of section 58

Add:

"A proposed law made under section 51A shall not be presented to the Governor-General for the Queen's assent until it has been passed by both Houses on two occasions—not less than six months apart."

3 At the end of section 99

Insert:

"unless the law is made under section 51A."

4 At the end of section 107

Insert:

"subject to section 51A."

5 At the end of section 111

Add:

"States may surrender powers

111A. The Parliament of a State may also surrender any power of the State to the Commonwealth; and upon such surrender, and the acceptance thereof by the Commonwealth, such power shall become part of the jurisdiction of the Commonwealth. Any law of the Commonwealth passed in accordance with such surrender shall be in addition to any proposed law passed in accordance with section 51A."

Notes on Constitutional Amendment Bill

Summary:

Arguments for the Proposed Constitutional Amendment:

The current constitutional arrangements for Commonwealth–state cooperation are unable to fully address the economic, environmental and social challenges of the twenty-first century.

Australia in the twenty-first century is handicapped by nineteenth-century judgments regarding which matters could be dealt with at a state level. The inter-colonial tensions of the 1890s are no longer a relevant rationale for those safeguards built into the constitution to protect the autonomy of the states.

The requirement for all the states to concur with Australia-wide legislation on matters regarded in the nineteenth century as having no federal significance is onerous and not in the best interests of all Australians.

The Commonwealth parliament needs to be able to legislate more efficiently to ensure that Australia is competitive in a global economy.

The proposed amendments include safeguards relevant to the twenty-first century to ensure that the Commonwealth does not lightly encroach on traditional state matters. Any proposed law on a traditional state matter must be passed by both houses on two occasions—not less than six months apart.

The consequential amendments in the Bill avoid internal conflicts in the constitution and also ensure that current provisions for Commonwealth–state cooperation are not affected—that is, if the states agree with Commonwealth action there would be no need to pass the Bill twice.

Background Notes

Commonwealth–State Cooperation—As Intended in 1901

In addition to the exclusive legislative powers of the Commonwealth (section 52), section 51 of the constitution confers legislative powers on the parliament over thirty-nine specified areas, some of which can be exercised concurrently with the states or with the permission of a state or states (for example, paragraph xxxiv).

Paragraph xxxvii of section 51 allows any state or states to refer a power to the Commonwealth; that is, the Commonwealth has always had a head of power to legislate on state matters, but only with the concurrence of any state affected by the law.

Chapter V of the constitution protects the autonomy of the states but acknowledges the need for Commonwealth leadership by providing that Commonwealth laws shall prevail in the event of any inconsistency (section 109).

The constitution provides indirect opportunities for the Commonwealth to exercise powers in areas of state legislative responsibility—for example, section 96 (financial assistance to the states).

Section 99 prevents the Commonwealth from giving preference to one state at the expense of the others in matters of trade, commerce or revenue.

Commonwealth–State Cooperation—As Seen in the Twenty-First Century

A complicated system of tied and untied grants to the states—motivated by practical necessity—has changed the relationship between the Commonwealth and the states envisaged by the drafters of the constitution.

The extension of the Commonwealth's powers has been influenced by recognition of changing circumstances requiring greater unanimity of laws as well as by the Commonwealth's greater financial strength.

High Court constitutional interpretation has also supported a wider interpretation of these powers than was envisaged by the drafters.

The Commonwealth has a strong legislative record in areas of traditional state responsibility such as education and health. The need to improve national standards in these and other areas supports a formal extension of Commonwealth legislative powers.

Current arrangements by which the Commonwealth (eventually) influences on areas of traditional state powers include intergovernmental agreements reached at COAG (Council of Australian Governments) meetings as well as at specialised intergovernmental forums (for example, the Standing Committee of Attorneys-General). These arrangements are unwieldy, inefficient and in many cases unsuccessful. They are not in the best interests of all Australians.

Challenges such as global environmental problems and the international economic outlook support greater opportunities for the Commonwealth to legislate for all Australians—with or without the concurrence and support of a state or states.

Notes

Introduction: Liberal Politicians Should Write More Books

1. Cameron, 'Practical Conservatism', p. 15.
2. Martin, p. 16.

1. The Making of a Liberal Politician

1. Scruton, 'The Usurpation of the State', p. 12.
2. Ibid., p. 13.

2. A Tale of Two Governments

1. Abbott, 'Health Care Agreements'.
2. Stone, 'Howard: Growth, Jobs, and Prosperity', p. 15.
3. Costello, p. 7.
4. Stone, 'Our Greatest Prime Minister', p. 12.
5. Bibby.
6. Kates, p. 7.
7. Murray, p. 8.
8. See Murray.

3. What's Right?

1. Santamaria, p. 21.
2. Quoted in Santamaria, p. 22.
3. Santamaria, p. 25.
4. Menzies, *Afternoon Light*, p. 287.
5. Roggeveen, p. 33.
6. Melleuish, p. 12.
7. Ibid., p. 18.
8. Ibid., p. 22.
9. Quoted in Melleuish, p. 20.
10. Menzies, *Afternoon Light*, p. 282.
11. Ibid., p. 286.
12. Menzies, *Speech Is of Time*, p. 219.
13. Abjorensen, p. 53.
14. Fraser.
15. Quoted in Henderson, p. 35.

16. Hayek, p. 398.
17. Quoted in Blake, p. 5.
18. Cameron.
21. Ray, p. xxv.
22. Blake, p. 359.
23. Ibid., p. 338.
24. Quoted in Blake, p. 363.
25. Quoted in Huntingdon, p. 465.
26. Quoted in O'Brien, p. 404.
27. Ibid.
28. Oakeshott, p. 178.
29. Ibid., p. 189.
30. Ibid., p. 174.
31. Ibid., p. 194.
32. Megalogenis.
33. Quoted in Johnson, 'What Is a Conservative?', p. 13.
34. Hayek, p. 399.
35. Ibid., p. 406.
36. Ibid., p. 409.
37. Raeder, p. 8.
38. Quoted in Scruton, 'Hayek and Conservatism', p. 212.
39. Johnson, 'What Is a Conservative?', p. 2.
40. Ibid., p. 3.
41. Quoted in Blake, p. 309.
42. Howard, 'Liberalisation in Economic Policy and Modern Conservatism in Social Policy'.
43. Howard, Melbourne Press Club address.
44. Quoted in Abjorensen, p. 134.
45. Abjorensen, p. 133.

4. Unfinished Business

1. Stone, 'Howard: Growth, Jobs, and Prosperity', p. 15.
2. Stone, 'Liberty, Productivity and Jobs'.
3. Costa, 'Unions May Yet Rue Rudd's IR Reforms'.
4. Harding et al., pp. 8 and 12.
5. Maley, p. 83.
6. Ibid., p. 85.
7. Ibid., p. 182.
8. Quoted in Sullivan, p. 3.

9. Sullivan, p. 18.
10. Ibid., p. 20.
11. Ibid., p. 26.
12. Ibid., p. 30.
13. Ibid., p. 31.
14. Ibid., p. 33.
15. Ibid., p. 10.
16. McDonald, p. 485.
17. Ibid., p. 487.
18. Turnbull, 'It's the Birth Rate, Stupid!', p. 5.
19. Ibid., p. 19.
20. Ibid., p. 24.
21. Payne, p. 11.
22. Ngu Vu and Harding.
23. *Hansard*, p. 338.
24. Saunders.
25. Harding et al., p. 1.
26. Institute of Actuaries, p. 22.
27. Productivity Commission, *Economic Implications of an Ageing Australia*, p. 334.
28. Asher, p. 21.

5. Australia's Biggest Political Problem and How to Fix It

1. See Brown.
2. Craven, 'Betrayal of Menzies'.
3. Hague, p. 10.
4. Ibid., p. 11.
5. Craven, 'Betrayal of Menzies'.
6. Quoted in Brown, p. 7.
7. Allen Consulting Group.
8. Wanna, p. 3.
9. Walker, p. 37.
10. Craven, 'An Unlikely Alliance'.
11. Howard, 'Reflections on Australian Federalism', p. 3.
12. Costa, 'First Aid Won't Suffice, Dr Rudd'.
13. Costa, 'Lingering Blame Game'.
14. Quoted in Parkin and Anderson, p. 105.
15. Howard, interview on radio 3AW.
16. Howard, 'Reflections on Australian Federalism', p. 3.

6. Making the States Do Better

1. Costa, 'Blame Labor's Hierarchy, Not Rees'.
2. Donnelly, p. 7.
3. Ferrari, p. 1.
4. See Loughnane, p. 21ff.
5. See Loughnane.

7. If the 2020 Summit Had Been Fair Dinkum ...

1. Howard, 'Keeping Faith with Our Common Values'.
2. Plimer.
3. Lomborg.

References

Abbott, Tony, 'Health Care Agreements', paper for open forum, 5 May 2008.
——'Reform with a Social Conscience', speech to Young Liberal conference, Unley, SA, 11 January 2003.
Abjorensen, Norman, *John Howard and the Conservative Tradition*, Australian Scholarly Publishing, 2008.
Allen Consulting Group, *Evaluation of COAG Initiatives for Full and Effective Mutual Recognition*, June 2008.
Asher, Anthony, 'Means Tests: An Evaluation of the Justice of Imposing High Rates of Clawback on Those of Modest Means', presentation to the Institute of Actuaries, 11 May 2006.
Australian Institute of Health and Welfare, *Geographic Variation in the Use of Dental Services, Research Report No. 41*.
Bibby, Paul, 'Sidetracked and Stuck in the Past', *The Sydney Morning Herald*, 19 April 2009.
Blake, Robert, *The Conservative Party from Peel to Thatcher*, Methuen, 1985.
Brown, AJ, 'What Should Australian Federalism Be Like in 2020?', address to the Future of Federalism conference, University of Queensland, 12 July 2008.
Cameron, David, 'Making Progressive Conservatism a Reality', 22 January 2009.
——'Practical Conservatism', Sir Keith Joseph Memorial Lecture, 2005.
Costa, Michael, 'Blame Labor's Hierarchy, Not Rees', *The Australian*, 8 May 2009.
——'First Aid Won't Suffice, Dr Rudd', *The Australian*, 28 November 2008.
——'Lingering Blame Game', *The Australian*, 5 December 2008.
——'Unions May Yet Rue Rudd's IR Reforms', *The Australian*, 20 March 2009.
Costello, Peter, *The Costello Memoirs: The Age of Prosperity*, Melbourne University Press, 2008.
Craven, Greg, 'An Unlikely Alliance', *Australian Financial Review*, 5 March 2005.
——'Betrayal of Menzies—Eschewing Federalism', *The Australian*, 1 March 2005.
Donnelly, Kevin, *Why Our Schools Are Failing*, Duffy and Snellgrove, 2004.
Ferrari, Justine, 'Teachers Bid to Downgrade Literature in National Curriculum', *The Australian*, 28 February 2009.
Fraser, Malcolm, 'Liberalism—the Philosophy that Shapes Government Policy and Actions', address to the South Australian Liberal State Council, 5 December 1980.

Garling, Peter, SC, *Final Report of the Special Commission of Inquiry: Acute Care Services in NSW Public Hospitals, Overview*, 27 November 2008.

Hague, William, 'Change and Tradition', speech to the Centre for Policy Studies, 24 February 1998.

Hansard, 27 March 1941.

Harding, Ann, et al., 'Improving Work Incentives for Mothers', Natsem paper to the 37th Australian Conference of Economists, Gold Coast, 1 October 2008.

Hayek, FA, 'Why I Am Not a Conservative', in *The Constitution of Liberty*, University of Chicago Press, 1960.

Henderson, Gerard, 'Fraserism: Myths and Realities', *Quadrant*, June 1983.

Hewson, John, 'Menzies and the 1990s', Sir Robert Menzies Lecture, 1990.

Howard, John, interview on radio 3AW, 24 March 2005.

——'Keeping Faith with Our Common Values', Irving Kristol Lecture, 2008.

——'The Liberal Tradition: The Beliefs and Values which Guide the Federal Government', Robert Menzies Lecture, 1996.

——'Liberalisation in Economic Policy and Modern Conservatism in Social Policy', address to Australia Unlimited Roundtable, 4 May 1999.

——Melbourne Press Club address, 22 November 2000.

——'Reflections on Australian Federalism', address to Menzies Research Centre, 11 April 2005.

Huntingdon, Samuel, 'Conservatism as an Ideology', *American Political Science Review*, June 1957.

Institute of Actuaries, *Discussion Paper on Retirement Incomes Reform*, August 2008.

Johnson, Paul, 'What Is a Conservative?', Centre for Policy Studies spring address, 1996.

——'Who Was the Most Right-Wing Man in History?', *The Spectator*, 26 February 2006.

Kates, Steven, 'The Dangers of Keynesian Economics', *Quadrant*, March 2009.

Kemp, David, 'Liberalism and Conservatism in Australia Since 1944', in B Head and J Walter (eds), *Intellectual Movements and Australian Society*, Oxford University Press, 1988.

Knox, David, *Pensions for Longer Life*, Committee for the Economic Development of Australia, 2007.

Lomborg, Bjorn, 'Green Energy a Better Bet', *The Australian*, 30 April 2009.

Loughnane, Brian, 'Doing What's Right for Australia', Liberal Party election material, October 2007.

McDonald, Peter, 'Low Fertility and the State', *Population and Development Review*, September 2006.

Maley, Barry, *Family and Marriage in Australia*, Centre for Independent Studies, 2001.

Martin, AW, *Robert Menzies, A Life*, vol. 2, Melbourne University Press, 1999.

Megalogenis, George, 'Nation Leans to the Left', *The Australian*, 11 April 2009.

Melleuish, Gregory, *A Short History of Australian Liberalism*, Centre for Independent Studies, 2001.

Menzies, RG, *Afternoon Light*, Cassell Australia, 1967.

——*Speech Is of Time*, Cassell London, 1958.

Murray, Kim, 'John Howard's Policies: Formed Over a Lifetime, so Why Were We Surprised?', paper to the Howard Decade conference, Canberra, 3 March 2006.

National Foundation for Australian Women, submission to the Productivity Commission Inquiry into Paid Maternal, Paternal and Parental Leave, 25 May 2008.

Ngu Vu, Quoc and Ann Harding, 'Winners and Losers from Tax-Transfer System and Other Changes during the Howard Years', presentation to the Future for the Australian Welfare State conference, Macquarie University, 25 July 2008.

Oakeshott, Michael, *On Being Conservative, Rationalism in Politics and Other Essays*, Methuen, 1981.

O'Brien, Conor Cruise, *The Great Melody*, University of Chicago Press, 1992.

Parkin, Andrew, and Geoff Anderson, 'Reconfiguring the Federation', in C Aulich and R Wettenhall (eds), *The Fourth Howard Government*, UNSW Press, 2008.

Payne, Alicia, et al., *Another Day, Another Dollar*, National Centre for Social and Economic Modelling, University of Canberra, 2007.

Plimer, Ian, *Heaven and Earth—Global Warming: the Missing Science*, Connor Court Publishing, 2009.

Productivity Commission, *Economic Implications of an Ageing Australia: Research Report*, 24 March 2005.

——*Paid Parental Leave Draft Inquiry Report*, 2008.

Raeder, Linda, 'The Liberalism/Conservatism of Edmund Burke and FA Hayek', *Humanitas*, vol. 10, no. 1, 1997.

Ray, John (ed), *Conservatism as Heresy*, Australia and New Zealand Book Company, 1974.

Roggeveen, Sam, 'Conservatism and Classical Liberalism—a Rapproachment', *Policy*, winter 1999.

Ryan, Siobhain, 'Ford Fears ETS Could Drive Jobs Out of Australia', *The Australian*, 21 April 2009.

Santamaria, BA, 'Reflections on Australia's Political Future', *Quadrant*, May 1985.

Saunders, Peter, *Expanding Low-Skilled Unemployment*, Centre for Independent Studies, 14 February 2008.

Scruton, Roger, 'Hayek and Conservatism', in E Feser (ed.), *The Cambridge Companion to Hayek*, Cambridge University Press, 2006.

——'The Usurpation of the State', *Quadrant*, November 1984.

——'Why I Became a Conservative', *The New Criterion*, vol. 21, no. 6, February 2003.

Stone, John, address to HR Nicholls Society, 27 March 2009.

——'Howard: Growth, Jobs, and Prosperity', *Quadrant*, January–February 2009.

——'Liberty, Productivity and Jobs: Workplace Relations under the Howard Government', *Quadrant*, July–August 2008.

——'Our Greatest Prime Minister', *Quadrant*, March 2008.

Sullivan, Lucy, *The Influence of Income Equity on the Total Fertility Rate*, Menzies Research Centre, 2003.

Turnbull, Malcolm, 'Green Carbon Initiative', address to Young Liberal Council, 24 January 2009.

——'It's the Birth Rate, Stupid!', address to National Population Summit, 21 November 2003.

Van Onselen, Peter (ed.), *Liberals and Power*, Melbourne University Press, 2008.

Walker, Geoffrey, 'Ten Advantages of a Federal Constitution', *Policy*, summer 2000–01.

Wanna, John, 'The Prospects for Federal Reform', paper for Institute of Public Administration Australia conference, September 2007.

Index

www.ingramcontent.com/pod-product-compliance
Ingram Content Group Australia Pty Ltd
76 Discovery Rd, Dandenong South VIC 3175, AU
AUHW011416150626
428608AU00030B/477

9 780522 864243